Finding
Home
a true story

KATHERINE APRUZZESE SHERBROOKE

ISBN: 0615518087
ISBN-13: 9780615518084

TO MY PARENTS,
who taught me that life
is exactly what we make it

Introduction

My father has always been an amazing storyteller. He has a Rolodex of jokes that would outlast most professional comedians, and recollections of his legal career and his life with my mother still amaze me with their vivid details. Whether it is the exact location of a hotel in Italy that my parents enjoyed on their first trip to Europe or the name of the gentleman who interviewed him for a clerkship role in 1953, my father's stories have always brought the experience to life for me. Particularly the story of my parents' romance, so turbulent and so inspiring. I was always proud of what my parents overcame in their own lives to become the people they are, and what they overcame during their love affair to create their own family, our family, and to own their own story.

I have for a very long time wanted to chronicle that story.

So I asked my father if I could spend some time with him and interview him—talk through all the old stories I had heard, many that I had not, and delve into the details of some of the more pivotal moments of their life together. I figured that hearing his thoughts and memories now was my only way to ensure that the details would not recede into the murky past with no way to break back up to the surface and into the light. I spent several days with him at my parents' house in Naples, Florida, tape recorder in hand, eagerly soaking in every last detail. Those conversations weren't my only source of material, however. It turns out that he had started to write much of this story several years earlier, and willingly shared those pages with me. In his own introduction he wrote, "There is a compulsion within me to do this. And so it is that I take pen in hand to recount our lifetime together..."

When my father says he took "pen in hand," he is being quite literal. And as my brothers and sisters can attest, my father's penmanship would challenge the most diligent code-crackers out there. Luckily, he patiently read his words out loud to me as I transcribed (and let the record show that even he had trouble deciphering his own scratch marks at times). While he didn't delve into nearly as much detail on those pages as I do here, those recollections serve as the foundation for this project.

Since those first few days together in Naples, my father has spent hours with me on the phone, reviewing every chapter multiple times, correcting errant facts, and peeling back ever more layers of key situations to help me capture them properly. We also took a tour of Newark together, visiting every important building of his youth and his early days with my mother.

I also did as much of my own research as possible to corroborate facts, describe particular places, or fill in missing details, diving into boxes of old family documents, and utilizing the vast frontier of information available online. But it goes without saying that this is my retelling of their story. I used my own paintbrush in this process, and while I relied heavily on my father to verify the authenticity of the various hues I chose, anything inaccurate is my mistake alone.

The fact that my father has handed over the stories of his life to me and has trusted me with the attempt to bring them to life on the page is incredible to me. I am humbled by that trust and hope that in the telling, my mother and father are able to forever dance together joyfully across the page.

CHAPTER ONE

Las Vegas

In May of 2007, my father arrives at the check-in counter of the Wynn Hotel in Las Vegas.

"How many keys would you like for your room, sir?"

"Just one," my father says.

He steps off the elevator and walks down the long hall, which curves slightly so as not to reveal exactly how long a journey it might be to the end. Pulling his suitcase over the lush maroon carpet, he drifts over to his left and briefly touches the molding on the wall. He has always had this habit of tapping various objects on the sidelines as he walks, as if verifying the confines of his surroundings. He swerves back to the right, his unsteady gait making the course correction look unplanned, and finds the white door with his room number on it.

As he sets his suitcase down to unpack, he is trying hard to feel the sense of relief that getting away is supposed to provide. Coming off the hardest months of his life, and having found no relief for his unrelenting sadness, he had hoped a quick trip might lighten his mood, or at least distract him for awhile from the day-to-day reality of life without his bride. His bride—a term he has used to refer to my mother for as long as I can remember.

In some ways, Las Vegas was such an odd choice for my father. Knowing he has traveled with my mother for over fifty years to some of the most beautiful and exclusive corners of the world, I would have expected him to choose somewhere like the San Pietro in Positano, perched on the cliffs of the Amalfi Coast. There he could gaze toward the horizon and seek solace in the waves and *la luna* that had shone down on them so many times over the years.

On the other hand, Las Vegas has a few advantages. It is full of distractions: Cirque du Soleil shows, great restaurants, dancing fountains, and, of course, miles of card tables and slot machines, not that he was ever a gambler. Most importantly, Vegas is a quick flight home were my father to get an emergency call about my mother.

Splashing water on his newly shaven face, hoping for a spark of energy or enthusiasm, he sees eyes in the mirror that are hazy and sapped of their spark. He rubs VO5 cream into his hair. His fingers disappear into his thick waves, now almost completely silver but for a hint of the jet black coif of his youth. He sits down on the upholstered bench at the end of the bed to put on his loafers and wonders what he is doing here, exactly. That moment's hesitation is like the unlatching of a screen door that gets immediately slammed open by the wind. His shoulders begin to shake, as has been happening so often lately. He has stopped fighting it, and lets the tears roll onto his face and drip on the carpet at his feet.

The crushing flickers of memories revolve in his mind and keep the screen door banging open, his body struggling to contain his grief.

Their fiftieth anniversary party almost two years earlier. He had planned it for months, selecting the invitations, securing the family photographer, finding the florist. Their friends came to Cape Cod from California, Oregon, Texas, New Jersey, Canada, and beyond to gather under the tent. My mother smiled and nodded at all the faces that congratulated them as he held her hand and guided her from group to group during cocktail hour. The wine was flown in from a friend's vineyard. The swordfish was succulent, the swing band even better. The sunset over the bay provided a warm orange and blue backdrop to heartfelt toasts and grandchildren singing. The crowning moment was a thirty-minute slide slow of their life, the perfect tribute. The next day, when a departing guest told her how much he had enjoyed the slide show, my mother said sweetly, "Oh? I don't think I saw that." She must have wondered that day why there were so many bare tables and folded up chairs strewn about her lawn.

The day he was trying to help her get into the shower back in Naples. Sometimes she willingly submitted, letting him wash her hair, drying her off with a plush white towel before putting the terry cloth robe around her shoulders. Sometimes laughing together as he combed her hair and helped her put on clean undies and pressed khakis. But on this day, she was resisting him. She didn't want to be touched. She didn't want to get into the shower.

"I want to go home!"

He thought she was just confused. "Sweetheart, we are home."

She is angry because he doesn't understand. "I want to go home!"

He now knows this is a common plea made by victims of dementia. It means she is searching for solace, yearning for a place of safety and comfort that she cannot find, a peace of mind that she cannot grasp. The idea of it threatens to starve him of oxygen.

3

The images of all the moments they will no longer be able to enjoy together won't stop crashing into him.

Finally, he takes a handkerchief out of the pocket of his blazer, wipes his face, and blows his nose. He takes a deep breath, stands up, checks his breast pocket for his bill fold, and slowly leaves the room. He has tickets to the latest Cirque show. He will not remember much about it. He has reservations at a highly touted restaurant owned by some famous New York chef. He won't remember the food. He will try the megabucks machines without any desire to have the flashing lights of a winning pull call him out to the crowd.

By his third day in Las Vegas, he is more exhausted then when he arrived. He has given up on the notion that simple distractions will help him escape. What continues to shatter all attempts at suppressing his anguish are the couples everywhere, gazing at each other across dimly lit tables, holding hands as they excitedly approach the gambling floor. He wonders if any of them are really in love. If any of them will have to make sacrifices to be together. If any of them will be as desperate as he is now, because they will be as lucky as he was then.

Maybe what he should do is try harder to remember. And he finds himself beside the pool at the Wynn, hotel stationery and Cross pen in hand. Finding a table in the shade, he sits, and begins to write.

> *As I write this, I am sitting by a pool at the Wynn Hotel in Las Vegas—all alone.*
>
> *Why did I come here? What moved me to take four days away from Naples, the Cape and my family? The only explanation I can give is that I wanted to break out of the confines that now engulf my life...*

4

There is a compulsion within me to do this. And so it is that I take pen in hand to recount our lifetime together, in order to better understand where we are and the import to our children and grandchildren, as well as those living through this agony, what it means. I may not reveal anything that hasn't already been set forth by others, but the experience is unique to me. It may have a therapeutic effect or it may only deepen the grief. Either way, it must come out as I wrestle with this problem.

Recount a lifetime. There is so much to tell. Where to start? Then he realizes that there is really only one story. The story of how they almost weren't together at all.

CHAPTER TWO

Their Meeting

My parents met in February of 1954, on a street corner in Newark, New Jersey. For some time they were embarrassed about this fact, and used to tell people otherwise, but as time wore on, I think they realized how perfectly that meeting snapped into place the image of their shared destiny.

My father was taking a break from studying for the New Jersey State Bar Exam, which he would take in June. He had walked down the street from his parents' apartment on Ardsdale Terrace to a local store to buy tobacco for his pipe, and was standing on the corner of South Orange Avenue, chatting with two other fellows. While he was never very good at smoking a pipe (in fact, he realized some time later that he is quite allergic to smoke), such was the fashion for a young man looking for a distraction from the ordeal of studying for the Bar.

A car pulled up to the curb with a beautiful young woman in the passenger seat, looking like she had just walked straight out of a L'Oreal commercial. Her skin was flawless, as if it had never had the chance to be damaged by the sun, yet she radiated the healthy flush of fresh-air adventure. She was holding a newspaper and was clearly in need of directions. My father edged out the other two chaps who were all drawn toward the car. Not only did he want to engage her in conversation, he was anxious to know who was driving the car. Was this beautiful woman already claimed by some lucky young man? She was not wearing a wedding band—a good sign. Leaning down a bit further, he saw, to his relief, an older man with very white hair at the wheel—her father. She looked up to ask her question.

She must have immediately noticed his incredibly thick head of hair. At twenty-five years of age, his hair was a deep shiny black with waves that would be hard to find nowadays outside of native-born sons in the old country. She could see a certain confidence that gave him a commanding presence. And his smile was impossible to miss, his square white teeth a crisp contrast to his olive skin. Also, Vin Apruzzese was always impeccably dressed; so even though he was on a study break, there is no doubt he was wearing a pressed shirt tucked into pleated pants with a complementary sweater vest and jacket to fight back the late winter chill.

"I'm hoping you can help," she said. "We are looking for the apartment advertised here and can't seem to find the right street."

He had a hard time breaking his gaze from her shimmering blue eyes to look at the address. He knew exactly where it was. But giving her directions would simply send her away.

"You know," he smiled, looking back into her eyes, "as luck would have it, my folks are building a new house and are just about to move out of their apartment, which is right up the street here. It might be exactly what you are looking for."

They were both still holding on to the newspaper, as if they hoped it would connect them somehow, even though they weren't touching.

He looked back into her eyes. "It's on the first floor of my Aunt Florence's house. I'd be more than happy to give you a call and arrange a visit."

"Oh, that would be wonderful," she said, glowing out the window. She reluctantly pulled the newspaper back into the car, but waited a beat before blinking away from his gaze. Tearing a corner off the page, she glanced at her father, and wrote down her phone number. The small bit of paper gave her the opportunity to graze his hand when she handed it back to him.

"Please be sure to call," she said, and then sent a knowing smile back out the window. "I'm sure my parents would love to see the apartment."

He stepped back from the car, smiling broadly. The car didn't move. They gazed at each other as if they both wanted nothing more than to occupy the space that stood between them. It took a few elongated seconds before Vin realized that the car wasn't stalled simply due to the magnetic force he was feeling.

"Oh," he finally conceded, "you want to keep going straight down this street and make your third left."

The next morning, Vin ran up the steps to the law office where he had been clerking for about six months. His three fellow law clerks were there already, comparing notes about the weekend.

"Fellas," Vin announced, waving the small piece of paper at them. "Yesterday, I secured the most important phone number of my life!"

Wasting no time, he called her that day, and arranged a date for Friday night at the Condor in Livingston, New Jersey. The Condor was a restaurant and nightclub housed in a beautiful mansion originally built as a private residence. Constructed by Italian stone masons in the 1920s, it was later renamed the Crystal Plaza due to the magnificent crystal chandeliers imported from Czechoslovakia that adorned the main dining room.

They sat at a banquette table that night overlooking the dance floor. From the moment they were seated, Vin had the irresistible urge to kiss his elegant date. He was mesmerized by her soft blond hair, with a single wave at her ears, curled under at the nape of her neck. Her skin was as exquisite as he remembered, her red lipstick emphasizing the perfect ivory tone of her face. She was stunning in every way, and he couldn't stop gazing at her.

My mother was born Marie Agnes Yeager. Her two closest friends in high school shared the same first name, so it was decided that one of them would remain Marie, one would be called Ria, and my mother, because of the color of her hair, would be called Sandy.

At the time she was working as the fitting model for David Crystal in New York City, a designer known for his cruise wear, separates, and dresses with bell-shaped skirts or slender silhouettes, all tailored around impossibly small waistlines. Like the other girls, Sandy modeled the latest fashions at runway shows or for couturier clients. Additionally, all the samples for the runway were made to "fit" her, her five-foot-seven frame, small waistline, and mild curve in her hips apparently a walking example of the ideal figure. When she wasn't being pinned and prodded by the David Crystal designers or walking the latest sportswear item down the catwalk, Sandy was constantly sorting through the boxes of scrap materials. She was quite a seamstress in her own right, and the designers often gave her leftover fabrics. This allowed her to make many of her own clothes out of the finest fabrics available at essentially no cost. She was also able to buy any of the David Crystal samples for 50 percent off the wholesale price. Given that these samples were literally made for her, she rarely turned down the chance. These custom-made clothes coupled with her own handmade outfits assured that she was always dressed to a T, a trademark of my mother's that endured long after her modeling career.

Given the circumstances of their meeting, the young pair had much to discuss. Why was she looking for an apartment? What was he doing on that street corner? And what did her father have to say about the young man who had coaxed their phone number from his daughter? As the couple was seated, however, the small band kicked into a tempting tune, probably Glenn Miller or Tommy Dorsey. Realizing that he could get that much closer to his date on the dance floor, Vin asked Sandy to dance.

How I used to love to watch my parents dance. I can safely say that my father is one of the best dance partners I have ever come across, and I adore getting the chance to swing about the floor with him to a Frank Sinatra tune. But watching them together was like magic. As a runway model, my mother could glide across a floor as if she were barely lifting her feet. And my father is an expert silent communicator, using a soft pull on the lower back or a quickening of his lead hand as a whispered forecast of the next step. They never bumped in too close to each other, nor did they ever separate too far on their trips around the dance floor. It always looked effortless as they smiled and gazed at each other, enjoying the rhythm and the mood. And whether on the way to or from the dance floor, my father would never miss a chance to hold my mother's hand, often raising it to his lips to give the back of her hand a kiss.

And so they danced that night, in between courses of food and conversation, and they both began to sense that this pairing

11

was something electric. During the breaks between dances, they did get to learn a lot about each other. They realized that they were both born and raised in Newark, New Jersey. Vin told of his aspirations as a lawyer and his hope of passing the Bar Exam in June. Listening intently, she could sense that his determination was founded in hard work. This plus an obvious intelligence made for a powerful combination.

"I have no doubt you will pass the Bar with flying colors," she told him with such a sincere look that it sent a pleasant vibration through his chest. Suddenly he was quite sure he would pass also.

When the conversation turned to Sandy, she told him that she had recently moved back home from California and was living with her parents, hence the need for a larger apartment. She had been pulled out West by a desire to see if her success modeling in New York might be transferred to the Hollywood scene. She had many glamorous stories to tell, but did not meander around meaningless details for long before telling her handsome date the most defining fact about herself.

"You should know that I have a four-year-old daughter named Barbara, and I am in the process of getting a divorce."

In most circles in 1954, this would have been cause for a painfully elongated, if not fatal, pause to a conversation. In Italian Catholic circles like Vin's, it was an absolute show-stopper.

Vin looked at her for a heartbeat or two before responding. "Would you like to dance?"

At that moment, Vin Apruzzese held two irreconcilable truths in his heart: that his parents—no, in reality, his father—would never approve of such a joining, and that he wanted to be with this woman. Conflict abounded. He knew immediately that the kind of discrimination he had been fortified against as a child would now cloud his own father's perceptions. As an Italian-American, his father always made it clear that he was "starting behind his own goal line." This was never stated as a complaint or an excuse, simply as a matter of fact. Accordingly, Vin was taught at an early age that success in life would hinge on his ability to work twice as hard as anyone else. Living that reality, however, had cemented for Vin the idea that every individual should be judged on their merits, not by their circumstance. Divorce was just an unfortunate circumstance.

But Vin also believed in the bond of family, a bond as strong as the roots that tether a towering oak to the ground. He had no desire to create a storm that would test the fortitude of those roots.

Beneath the sparkling crystal chandeliers at the Condor, Vin gave over to his heart and his undiminished desire to kiss Sandy and bring her into his life. She willingly obliged. When they walked off the dance floor, he held her hand. He did not let it go after they sat down.

"How is the apartment search going?" he asked.

She laughed. "That was quite a resourceful way to get my number in front of my father!"

"It did the trick," he replied, smiling. "And my aunt's apartment really is for rent. But tell me what you are looking for. I also have a few buddies in the area who might know of something that's available. I'd be happy to call them for you if that would help."

She could sense a man who was used to getting things done and helping other people in their efforts to accomplish something whenever he could. She liked that. "I think my father has a lead on a nice apartment in Belleville. But thank you, Vin."

No one had ever called him Vin before. He was always Vinny to his cousins. And his work colleagues had taken to calling him

13

Vince. But she claimed the name Vin for him, and he would never be anything else in her world.

They spent the rest of the evening talking, learning more about each other, swinging around the dance floor, and becoming ever more certain that love was pulling them in close.

After delivering Sandy back to her parents' apartment, Vin knew that the glimpse he had had of a looming storm could not be ignored. As much as his young heart believed that love could and should break down any unfair conceptions one individual might have about another, especially one as lovely as this incredible woman, he knew in this same heart that his father would never approve.

CHAPTER THREE

Young Romance

This wouldn't be the first time that Vin's father wouldn't approve of his son's romantic intentions. Vin became involved with his first real girlfriend, Mary Kwasek, during his senior year of high school. She was a competitive swimmer and diver (another woman with a figure to be envied) and planned to study to become a nurse. They went out on fairly regular dates, not something young Vin was willing to share with his parents. As he says, "The idea of being involved with a girl while in high school? Forget it. They would have gone ballistic." His parents' feeling that romance was not something their young son should as yet entertain created a telling situation during Vin's senior year of high school that served as a harbinger of the future.

My father is quite accomplished on the piano. While he was clearly born with significant musical aptitude, he has his father to thank for his training. He was required to practice for at least one hour every day from the age of seven straight through high school, even on holidays and Sundays. His father was quite clear on this account. If the sun suddenly broke through on a rainy afternoon and other boys were knocking at the window, there would be no running outside to play football or baseball in the street until the piano had been played for a full hour. There was a Big Ben alarm clock on top of the piano to ensure that the full hour was fulfilled. On the plus side, the alarm also ensured that no practice session would last a minute past the hour, either. Painful as it was, it worked. To this day my father can light up a room just by sitting down at the piano and can get even the stodgiest guest at a cocktail party to break into song.

In high school, Vin played with the school band and accompanied the school's a cappella choir. Their senior year he was invited to participate in a huge Christmas performance at the Mosque Theater in Newark. This was quite an honor. The Mosque Theater, which would later become the New Jersey Symphony Hall, boasted a seating capacity of more than twenty-eight hundred, a seventy-foot-wide stage, and near-perfect acoustics. It would eventually be graced by all the greats of the day, including Frank Sinatra, Judy Garland, Benny Goodman, and even the Rolling Stones in 1965. But on this occasion, in December of 1945, it was host to the New Jersey All-Star Chorus, involving more than eight hundred students from across the state. The crowning performance was to be the Hallelujah Chorus, with Vincent Apruzzese front and center, at the piano.

What a moment of pride for his parents! To see all that diligent work pay off for their son in such a majestic setting with throngs of people able to appreciate his prowess at the piano. The only catch was that Vin didn't invite his parents. The equation was quite simple. Like any smitten young man, he wanted Mary to be there to see his grand performance and then take her out for a celebratory date afterward. He knew this innocent desire could not be fulfilled if his parents were there, and so he never told them about the concert.

Vin and Mary continued to date all through college. He would come home every weekend to help at his father's tavern and to see Mary. And while his mother by then had met Mary on occasion, his father never had. As my father says, "My dad was always working. He would start at seven in the morning and would come home at six at night, and then he was tired. And I never had a free and easy relationship with my father where if you had a girl you could bring her by. I never minded telling my mother, but she was always guarded; what was my father going to say?"

During his senior year of college, Vin figured it was probably time to get married. Mary had successfully made it through nursing school, and he was going to enter law school. She had been patiently waiting for the next step and the timing seemed right. His father, however, still believed that romance, and in this case marriage, should not be a priority. Law school is a huge responsibility, and marriage might simply get in the way of future professional success.

He put it a little differently.

"You want to get married?" his father said. "Then forget it, I'm finished with you. You're on your own."

I can see young Vin raising his eyebrows, pulling his hands off the table between them, and leaning back into his chair, feeling a bit deflated by the force of this reaction.

"But I'll tell you what," his father continued. "Why don't you go ahead and get engaged? Just don't get married yet. I'll even buy the ring if you wait until you get through law school. Then you can get married." With his ever-present desire to protect his son, coupled with a truly generous side that was never far from the surface, Vin's father successfully managed to facilitate an engagement and put the brakes on a marriage all in one fell swoop. The engagement didn't survive the first year of law school.

As strong as his father's reaction was to Mary Kwasek, it was nothing compared to the fury he unleashed when Vin told him about Sandy.

"A divorced woman? With a child? Why would you do that to us? Why would you throw everything away that you have worked so hard for?"

Vin was dismayed. While he knew his father was not likely to embrace the situation, he nonetheless had held out hope that his father would be rational, or at the very least be swayed by his son's feelings. Vin was a grown man now and a law school graduate. Couldn't his father support his good fortune at having met the most marvelous young woman?

His father made clear from the start that any union between his son and a divorced woman would be nothing short of disastrous, so there was no need to pursue her. Any attempt to dissuade his father of his preconceptions on the situation just made matters worse. His father was steadfast in his conviction and was adamant that Vin should simply forget he had ever met Sandy. And if he turned his back on his father's wishes and the relationship became serious, there was no mistaking the consequence—Vin would face being disowned by his family.

But Vin could not quell his desire to be with Sandy, and did not attempt to hide this fact from his parents. The arguments that ensued would quickly erupt, all starting and ending in pretty much the same place. Whenever Vin would let his parents know that he would not be home for dinner because he had a date with Sandy, his father's disapproval would flood the room, the same indignant phrases surging into his anger again and again.

"Why would you throw away everything you have worked so hard for for a divorced woman with a child?"

Vin would try to convince his father that he wasn't throwing anything away. Sandy was Catholic, as were they, so religion wasn't a problem. As for her previous marriage, Vin saw his logic as quite simple. She had not been married in a church, therefore the Catholic Church did not recognize her first marriage. Surely the church would bless a second marriage. So why couldn't his father? Logic was not to win the day. Vin's father simply "could not fathom how his only progeny could do this to him."

Vin's mother deplored these heated debates. She had lost most of her hearing during a miscarriage shortly after Vin was born, and her early-model hearing aid required her to become fairly proficient at lip-reading. After a few of these arguments, however, she could almost follow with her eyes closed. The argument was always the same. She would have given anything to end the fighting, but she was, as my father puts it, "conflicted and unable to manage her recalcitrant husband."

Vin would frequently ask his father to agree to at least meet Sandy. Surely one minute in the room with such a loving and thoughtful woman would put his father's fears to rest. His father refused. As tempers continued to rise, Vin's father would sit down and put a little white nitroglycerine pill on his tongue. He had a heart condition that the doctor warned should not be tested with too much excitement or stress. The little white pill was like a white flag reluctantly raised. It put an unsatisfying end to the argument every time. Exacerbated, Vin would leave the room, furious that he could not make his father see his side.

Sunken in his chair, waiting for the little white pill to dissolve, Vin's father was stricken with anxiety. He was sure that his son was teetering on the edge of a huge mistake. He had worked so hard all these years to give his son a chance at a good life. And Vincenzino, as he often called his son, had understood how much diligence was required to succeed against the odds. After all, he had been such a conscientious student, a respectful and focused young man, and had followed his parents' wishes in every way. Hadn't he reaped the rewards of that? Hadn't he made it all the way through law school, and didn't he now have the chance at the kind of life any immigrant's son would envy? Why, then, would he voluntarily want to risk all that he had achieved by being with a divorced woman? And to make matters worse, a woman whose divorce would never go unnoticed or forgotten because she had a child? How could he so easily forget where he had come from? The more Vin's father thought back on his own life, the more it strengthened his resolve to stop his son from throwing everything away.

CHAPTER FOUR

Giovanni

Giovanni Apruzzese was born in Puglia, Italy, in 1897 in the town of Ascoli Satrianno. A recent veteran of WWI, he sailed alone at the age of twenty-three on the boat called America from Naples, Italy, to Ellis Island. He arrived in the new country on December 30, 1920, eagerly recording his height on the manifest at five-foot-six, a hopeful stretch for this small man who arrived with no high school education and spoke no English. His brother Luigi had come before him and was living in Roanoke, Virginia, where Giovanni would join him.

Contrary to my understanding as a child, the spelling of Apruzzese with a "p" was not the doing of some distracted manifest officer at Ellis Island who didn't bother to record names properly. While the region of Abruzzo has sprouted many families by the name Abruzzese, just to the south of this region in Puglia, where Giovanni was raised, there were many families that spelled their name with a "p." And so the Apruzzese name was not an invention of carelessness, but a true representation of ancestry.

In Virginia, Giovanni took a job cutting hair in a shop next to Hollins University. The hair permanent was new in those days, and it took great skill to create the perfect "finger wave" for delighted female clients. Giovanni took to the profession quite quickly.

It was on a trip to Newark, New Jersey, for his good friend Salvatore Russo's wedding that Giovanni would meet his future wife. It was not long after that he decided to settle in Newark and open up his own barber shop.

Vin's parents' marriage was not the stuff of romance novels, but perhaps would fit more comfortably in a practical handbook of the day for how to find a spouse and build a family together. With one odd exception—it seems that they were married twice.

Emelia Cerefice, who always went by the name Mildred, was one of eleven children. Like all of her older brothers and sisters, she went to work directly after finishing eighth grade to help support the family. Her father had died young, and multiple paychecks were needed to keep the coal burning for a family of twelve. Mildred's mother, always called Nonna by my father, ruled the house like a drill sergeant, very clear what had to be done to keep the house running and everyone fed each day. And, of course, a major responsibility of hers was seeing that her daughters found suitable husbands.

Mildred was a beautiful woman. Giovanni took to her right away at the Russo wedding, but it is unclear that the feeling was entirely mutual. The Italian man with the sweet smile had ears that were rather a bit too large for his head, and he was several inches shorter than Mildred. But Nonna knew a hardworking and respectable man when she saw one and thought Mildred should take a deeper look.

Courtship was a bit clumsy in those days as being together without a chaperone was not for proper girls. Nonna always insisted on having one of Mildred's sisters accompany the couple on dates. Before long, Giovanni asked Nonna's permission to marry her daughter. It seems that permission was granted without Mildred being entirely convinced of the idea because, although the pair was married in a civil ceremony, they did not live together at first. They were now able to date unchaperoned, and perhaps the ability to get to know each other unhampered by the watchful eyes of another showed Mildred the soft heart of this man. Or maybe it simply became clear that a more committed version of marriage was the only realistic option. Whatever the ultimate impetus, they were married a second time with a "real" wedding and a shared household to go with it.

By this time Giovanni, eager to integrate as much as possible into the new world, was going by the anglicized name John and was running his own hair salon in East Orange. He catered to sophisticated women who desired permanents and the other high-end styles of the day and to businessmen who would stop in on their way to or from their Wall Street offices. But as the Great Depression sunk in, the women shifted their spending from trendy hairstyles to paying the butcher's bill. Then his Wall Street clients started to pass by the shop, overdue for a fresh cut but claiming that they could not stop because they would be late for their train.

Seeing the writing on the wall, John decided to move his operation to Market Street in Newark, and to offer basic barbershop haircuts for twenty-five cents each. There was still considerable competition even at that price. A barber college a few doors down offered cuts for only fifteen cents to anyone willing to submit their locks to the shears of an apprentice. The rent on the barber shop was one hundred dollars a month, or four hundred haircuts' worth of revenue. John took home about twenty-five dollars per week, the same amount received by those taking government assistance at the time—not an option John Apruzzese was ever willing to consider.

Vin was expected to help out with the business whenever possible. At twelve years old, he would take the bus with his father on weekends to the barber shop. He would spend the days sweeping up the hair from under the barber chairs and working the register for his dad.

An entrepreneur at heart, and wanting to get more out of the barber business, John invented a hair tonic he called *Mor Life*. As time permitted, he would drive around Newark and into New York City in his rumble-seat Chevy and try to sell his tonic to other hair salons and barber shops. Young Vin watched him design the sunburst label at the kitchen table. John had an interesting marketing angle for his concoction. While most hair tonic smells very pleasing, his did not, which he would use as the basis for his proof statement: "It doesn't smell nice like those other ones, but that's what makes it work!" While he didn't have enough paying customers who agreed, John did eventually sell his less-than-booming hair tonic franchise to Wildroot, a large consumer products company specializing in hair product and creams. As it turns out, they bought his fledgling tonic business not for the pungent solution but for the label, and went on to market one of their own tonics using his homemade sunburst design.

No longer needing traveling salesman transport, John didn't have a car again until some ten or twelve years later. Vin would actually have to reteach his father to drive, an experience that made him seriously question how his father had ever navigated the streets of New York City. Fortunately, to get from his home at that time in East Orange into Newark, John could drive the six miles straight down South Orange Avenue, requiring no turns. This made Vin feel much better about the idea of his father commuting by car.

After the sale of *Mor Life*, not ready to give up on opportunities to augment his income from the barber shop, John decided in 1934 to buy into a new ice cream franchise with Tom Bergamosco, the husband of Mildred's sister Louise. The franchise had a patent for serving ice cream from a novel ready-made paper cone, making the process of filling an ice cream cone much faster and easier. They opened up their store on Springfield Avenue in Newark, a very busy thoroughfare, and sold eighteen flavors of homemade ice cream. They called the store Eat More Ice Cream, and for a short time it was a hit. In fact, it was so popular that Woolworth's across the street closed their ice cream counter rather than compete. But running the ice-cream parlor as a part-time venture was a strain on the two partners. And when the franchiser lost its patent for the paper serving cone, removing the novelty and speed of the serving process, the two partners decided to close Eat More Ice Cream.

With these two side ventures behind him, John became increasingly clear that he wanted to throw his energy into a singular endeavor with greater potential than the barber shop. John's brother-in-law Al Paolini, married to Mildred's younger sister Jean, owned a building with his father at 378 Market Street in Newark, across the street from the Pennsylvania Railroad Station. They had a liquor license for the space and were anxious to sell a half share in the tavern business. They knew John had a very strong business sense and thought he would be the perfect person to help make the tavern successful. John thought the location was ideal for a watering hole and in 1941 decided to shut down his barber shop and buy into the business.

The Market Street Building was three stories high with apartments on the second and third floors. Al and Jean lived on the third floor. John had put every dime he had into the business, and the only way he could make the venture work financially was to move his family to the second-floor apartment.

At the time, John, Mildred, and Vin were living in the Vailsburg section of Newark, considered a relatively nice section of town. In the age-old aspiration in all communities to be on the "right side of the tracks," moving to Market Street, in the heart of the Iron Bound District, was decidedly going the wrong way. The Ironbound District was not so lovingly referred to in that day as "Down Neck" and not the place a mother hopes to raise a young son.

The new apartment on Market Street had four rooms that were set up railroad-style, eliminating any possibility of privacy for anyone. The bathroom had a toilet, with two wash basins outside the bathroom door. There was no shower or bath tub, which meant a trip across the street to Penn Station was necessary for the privilege of then paying for a shower. Their only outdoor space was a concrete slab outside the tavern's kitchen, which could hardly be considered a backyard. Vin's daily piano practices could be heard by the tavern regulars, causing frequent ribbings for the boy after particularly enthusiastic renditions of Chopin or Mozart. Vin's weekend work shifted from sweeping up hair and working the register to washing glasses, cleaning the mirrors behind the bar, and scrubbing the bathrooms. He was also tasked with helping his father make sausage, one hundred and fifty pounds at a clip. Mildred and her sister Jean worked in the kitchen, making meatballs, sausage and pepper sandwiches, and spaghetti for the customers. Vin and his family ate this same fare for dinner each night, gathering at a small table in the tavern's kitchen. There was an endless stream of dirty dishes that needed to be washed by hand every night, additional work Vin did not much enjoy.

These drawbacks were palpable, but there were more important things than location that Vin would miss. From the time he was born, Vin's Vailsburg home had been a four-family house at 102 Grand Avenue shared with Nonna and several of Mildred's siblings. Uncle Lou, Mildred's younger brother, lived in Nonna's apartment on the first floor across the hall from Vin and his family. Nonna's daily pot of chicken soup always piqued Vin's appetite, and he would sneak across the hall to pilfer a spoonful or two whenever Nonna was otherwise occupied. Aunt Mary and her husband, Uncle Louie, lived in one of the second-floor apartments with their four children, one of whom, Gloria, sometimes took a bit of the daily drudgery out of Vin's piano practice by playing duets with him. Gloria would eventually attend Juilliard, an option that Vin resisted when suggested to him by their mutual teacher. The fourth apartment was home to Aunt Florence, her husband Uncle Jim, and their two children. The group swelled even larger when Uncle Dick, out of work during the Depression, came to live in Nonna's apartment with his four daughters. So while Vin was technically an only child, he grew up feeling like he had a gaggle of siblings.

While the living arrangements might have been less than ideal for the adults, my father still remembers those days, Depression and all, with great affection. Whenever work was available, all of the adults, except Nonna and Aunt Florence, worked; Nonna ruled the house just as she had with her own children and was instrumental in helping get all the kids off to school in the morning. With so many kids and not much money to go around, my father remembers the games they would make out of mealtime on the occasions when they would all gather in Nonna's apartment for a meal. Nonna would put a huge wooden board in the center of the kitchen table covered in polenta with a few meatballs and sausages in the middle. The rule was that you could not eat the meat until you ate your way through the polenta. The cousins would each dig a tunnel to the center with their spoons, hoping to get to a sausage or meatball before being intercepted by another eager spoon.

On lucky days, Mildred would bring home candy from her job on the manufacturing line at the Charms Candy Company in Bloomfield, New Jersey. The favorite of all the kids was a chocolate bar wrapped in gold-leaf paper, called the "24 Carat." The cousins would anxiously wait until no adults were around and pry open the dining room cabinet in Vin's apartment to get at the sequestered goodies. And when Uncle Dick finally did get work, for a time he was a driver for Dugans bakery company. After delivering fresh-baked goods on his route, he was responsible for bringing the day or two old cupcakes and pies that hadn't sold back to the bakery. Sometimes, several of those treats would "fall off the truck" and end up in the hands of the delighted cousins.

Vin's favorite uncle was Uncle Don, Mildred's youngest brother, and only the second of Mildred's siblings allowed to continue beyond grammar school. His graduation from the University of Minnesota placed him in rarified air in Vin's world. A fellow piano player, he graduated as an officer in the ROTC. While working at the Sandy Hook base in New Jersey after graduation, Don would occasionally bring several of the cousins to the base for the weekend. On those trips, Vin was struck by the treatment of officers like Uncle Don, particularly the excellent food they were served, one of many signals to Vin over the years that it would be far better to serve as an officer than an enlisted man. Uncle Don would also take several of the cousins ice skating at South Mountain Reservation or to nearby parks in the summer when he was dating his future wife, Grace. Grace and Don would surreptitiously disappear while the kids were busy playing, and Vin relished being complicit in his uncle's courting of his beautiful bride-to-be.

Making family wine was an annual ritual. Several of the cousins would ride down to the markets with Uncle John and Uncle Louie to buy wholesale grapes, making several trips to get the whole load home. John and Louie would make up their wine recipe and lock away a barrel for each family in the basement to ferment. Uncle Jim was known to sneak into the basement and dip into his stash a bit early every year, the same Uncle Jim who would often go fishing and claim that his meandering swagger upon returning was surely due to "all that salt air." John also kept a small barber chair in the basement. When the cousins weren't pulling their sleds around the cement floor to sharpen the blades for a coming snowstorm, he would, of course, cut everyone's hair.

But with the recovery from the Depression, many things were changing. Aunt Florence and Uncle Jim were the first to move out. Uncle Jim's ability to maintain his job at the Public Service Electric and Gas without interruption during the Depression made them the "well-to-do" ones of the family. They moved to their own house on Hillcrest Terrace in East Orange. While the new house was only a few blocks away, the change of zip code was a leap across another invisible set of tracks, this time in the right direction. They capped this off with the purchase of a brand-new 1939 Pontiac, which widened Vin's eyes quite a bit upon first sight.

Aunt Mary and Uncle Louie then moved out as well, to Munn Avenue, also not far from Grand Avenue. This came on the heels of Nonna's death, something my father remembers vividly. His child's mind sees most clearly the open casket at his

Aunt Mary's house. There was a traditional small wooden box into which those who had come to pay their respects could put money to help the family. The family kept a running "book" of these donations, so they could readily reciprocate these offerings when the next relative passed on. While these traditions were meant to bring comfort and closure, they were nonetheless difficult for Vin to understand, and were not rituals he would cherish or choose to repeat.

So while life evolved, taking pieces of the colorful Cerefice family puzzle and pushing them into their own separate boxes for reasons having nothing to do with the tavern, my father's particular part of the evolution left much to be desired.

Beyond the many challenges of the move to be overcome, perhaps the most important was that Vin still had one year to go at the Alexander Street School before moving on to high school. Moving to Market Street put him in the wrong school district to complete his eighth-grade year. Because he was doing very well in school and was voted class president, no one thought that switching schools at that juncture was a good idea. So Vin used his Aunt Mary and Uncle Louie's new address on Munn Avenue as his "residence" so that he could finish elementary school.

His daily commute back across the tracks, however, made an important impression on the thirteen-year-old boy. The public bus full of commuters that Vin took to get back to his old neighborhood passed by the Essex County Courthouse, a formidable and stately white building constructed from seven thousand tons of raw marble. Eight elegant columns support a mantle that holds nine statues, each representing an aspect of the law, such as Reason and Protection. In front of the building is a wonderful sculpture of Abraham Lincoln, by Gutzon Borglum of Mount Rushmore fame. Lincoln is seated at one end of a bench. His right hand is placed on the empty spot on the bench, as if beckoning the onlooker to come and sit beside him. What made the biggest impression on Vin, however, were the words etched into three stone rectangles at the top of the building. He would read these words every day:

Laws are the very bulwarks of liberty
Justice renders to everyone his due
Be merciful as well as just

Gazing out of the bus window, he declared to himself every day that he would someday become a lawyer.

CHAPTER FIVE

The Road To Law

I t was a long road from the wrong side of the tracks in Newark to a career practicing law. Yet while so many things seemed to be conspire against him in the early days, I always had the impression that my father had complete confidence in his ability to beat the odds. When he relates, for example, how he was completely unaware of the process involved in applying for college until his Latin teacher mentioned an available scholarship to Rutgers, he sounds a bit incredulous. Not at his good fortune for having been singled out by this teacher as a worthy candidate, but at the remarkable reality that he was inches from falling behind.

I suppose success makes every lucky moment look fated and makes determination seem like the obvious choice, but in the heat of the moment, my father simply seized every opportunity presented to him. Then, heeding his father's wise words, he worked twice as hard as anyone else. My father's eventual success running his own labor law firm seems like a given now, but there were many twists in the road to contend with along the way.

Vin headed off to Rutgers in 1946, one of only twelve students in his class of two hundred and fifty from East Side High School in Newark to attend college. He was class president at East Side High, was awarded the Roster of Superior Merit (given to the top student in the class), and won a Special Award for Outstanding Musicianship. Despite these accolades, my father often says that he only learned "half of the alphabet" at East Side High, and so while he received an academic scholarship to Rutgers, he nonetheless wound up in remedial English upon arrival. The absence of college preparation also ensured that the only time he had previously stepped foot on a college campus was when his high school baseball team played against the plebes at West Point. The fact that their team was good enough to compete against college freshmen was pretty impressive considering the absence of athletic facilities at East Side High. The team's only place to practice was in the stadium parking lot of the Newark Bears, the New York Yankee's minor league team. The East Side team did get one chance to play inside the stadium, however, when they made it into the state championship, and won. Walking back across that parking lot with victory in hand gave them all a unique sense of pride.

As a land grant university, Rutgers required all freshmen to join ROTC for two years. They were then given the option of remaining in ROTC for their third and fourth years to earn officer status. Remembering his trips to the Sandy Hook base with his Uncle Don, and determined if ever called to duty to have the ranking of an officer, Vin accepted the option.

The advent of the GI Bill meant that in the fall of 1946, Vin was surrounded by veterans who had just returned from the war, swelling his incoming class from a typical size of three hundred to over eleven hundred students. Pre-fab buildings were erected along the banks of the Raritan River to house classrooms and a huge cafeteria. Housing was at a premium, forcing Vin to commute from Newark for the first several months of college before finding a bedroom to rent in nearby Highland Park. These physical alterations to campus life, coupled with the rash of inexperienced teachers that needed to be hired, made Rutgers feel less like a college campus than a factory for bachelor's degrees.

Vin's college experience was also tempered by the fact that he left campus every Friday afternoon to return home and help his dad at the tavern over the weekend. It was a quick commute, and he knew that his father relied on his help, especially once he had become a sole partner in the tavern business. John and Al Paolini's partnership had been strained almost from the start. Six months after opening the tavern, the attack on Pearl Harbor and the start of the war meant that Pennsylvania Railroad Station was booming with servicemen coming and going and countless workers who were needed to keep the station running smoothly. John saw an opportunity and wanted to invest in expansion with ideas like buying televisions to bring in bigger crowds and procuring liquor in greater quantities to reduce unit costs. Al saw such expenditures as overly aggressive, and the two rarely agreed. By 1947, it was clear that one partner would have to buy the other out. As the owner of the building, Al figured he couldn't lose. If John bought the license, he would still have to rent the space from him, allowing Al to continue to benefit somewhat from the success of the business. Unbeknownst to Al, however, John had purchased the building next door. After buying Al out of his tavern license and renovating his new space, John moved the newly renamed John's Tavern from 378 to 376 Market Street. Needless to say, John and

Mildred's relationship with her sister and Al Paolini did not survive that maneuver.

Weekend responsibilities aside, Vin managed to get involved in campus life, participating in various clubs and intramural sports, and setting up several businesses on campus. First he attempted to sell a line of college-branded hats with his good friend Tony "Docky" Doganiro at football games, not knowing that a permit was needed to sell such items at the stadium. An officer who put a stop to Vin's selling activities agreed to play a joke on Docky by driving over to Docky's side of the stadium with Vin in the back of his cruiser and announce that they were both under arrest. Docky didn't find this nearly as funny as his friend. Undeterred by this first hiccup, the duo then set up a co-op to sell school books at discounted rates. Vin also had a little jewelry business, offering everything from cuff links and tie clips to engagement diamonds, especially relevant to the older GIs on campus. Additionally, he and Docky, noting that there were no suitors lining up to recruit them for any of the over-run fraternities on campus, decided with several equally un-pursued black athletes that an integrated fraternity would be a good idea. Bucky Hatchett, an All-American football and basketball player, had been approached by the Omega Psi Phi Fraternity about starting a local chapter at Rutgers, and with that, the push for a new brotherhood on campus was born. The group set about recruiting members and began to host small picnics and other social events for the brothers and their dates. Vin was elected president and went with his other new brothers to the swearing-in ceremony at a major chapter in Newark. After learning their "secret handshake," Vin and Docky realized with some surprise that they were the only two white faces bobbing in a sea of black ones, having had no idea that Omega Psi Phi had been heretofore an entirely black organization. Despite the positive press that this newly integrated fraternity sparked, the group was never able to recruit the full twenty-man roster required to be officially recognized on campus. After the founding members graduated, the fraternity ceased to exist at Rutgers.

Vin graduated as a second lieutenant in the Air Force Reserve in the spring of 1950, ten days before the start of the Korean war. He matriculated to law school at the University of Pennsylvania that fall, but knew his studies could be interrupted at any time because of his five-year ROTC commitment. During Easter break of his second year, he and all nine of his Air Force ROTC law school classmates received orders to report to active duty. The night before the Federal Taxation Exam, all nine of them were given a last-minute option to delay their call to active duty in return for elongating their ROTC commitment from five to eight years. All nine accepted, and after a celebration in Philadelphia that went into the wee hours, Vin was "barely able see the paper" of the Federal Taxation Exam he took the next day. Fortunately, that one failing grade did not too badly damage his overall transcript.

The next telegram came during Easter break of Vin's third and final year, this time with orders to report directly after graduation. In order to practice law in New Jersey, Vin knew he was required to clerk at a law firm for nine months before sitting for the Bar exam. This call to duty would clearly delay fulfillment of this requirement, but he had no choice in the matter. So unlike the other third-year law students who were aiming for a career in New Jersey, Vin did not spend his spring term looking for a clerkship position. In early June, however, President Eisenhower cut back the defense budget, delaying his orders once again. Suddenly, Vin found himself newly graduated, with no officer position and no clerkship. He went overnight from starting behind his own goal line to being outside the stadium altogether.

Vin immediately set out to find a clerkship. He quickly identified the most established law firms in the area with good reputations and set about meeting with as many as possible, all to no avail. The only firm that showed any promise was Lum, Fairlie & Foster, a respected firm of about twenty-six lawyers. It was the oldest law firm in New Jersey and the only major firm in the state to have Italian partners, brothers Joe and Vin Buinno. Vin interviewed with a lawyer named Edmund Mancusi Ungaro. Mr. Ungaro was extremely encouraging to young Vin, impressed by his resume and demeanor, sincerely telling him that he surely would have hired him had he applied sooner. He simply had no space on his four-man clerkship roster. But he gave Vin the names of some additional firms he thought might be good options. And he kindly suggested removing several firms from Vin's list, as they would be unlikely to speak to, let alone employ, an Italian. This newly refined list totaled twenty-two law firms. Vin had no luck at any of them.

Deciding to cut his losses before the entire summer became unproductive, Vin opened a parking lot in Wildwood with his college friend Bill Gimello, making money from all the beach-goers who needed a place to park while they visited the Shore. While not particularly beneficial to his legal career, Vin made more money that summer parking cars than he would make clerking for an entire year. I sometimes wonder what other business enterprises my father might have created if his entrepreneurial instincts had continued to rule the day. But his desire to practice law was undiminished.

September brought better luck on the clerkship front. A very small firm, Lesnik, Amoscato & Gordon, headed by three Harvard Law grads, needed some help. Phil Gordon offered Vin a role during their interview on a Thursday, and asked if

Vin could start the next day. Amazed and appreciative of the opportunity, he accepted. During his first day on the job, Vin thought it important to see Mr. Ungaro from Lum, Farlie to advise him of his new employment status and thank him for all his help and encouragement. He purposely took his lunch break late in the day so that he could walk over to Mr. Ungaro's office at a time when he'd be likely to catch him. Upon seeing Vin, Ungaro's face lit up.

"You won't believe it," he said. "I just had a new clerk tell me that he has to leave because his wife, who is from the South, is unhappy here and wants to move back home. I have a space for you. Can you come clerk for us?"

Vin was dumbfounded. Not knowing what he should do, he called on two people for counsel, Judge Cafiero, the father of a law school classmate and someone whom he trusted deeply, and his own father. The judge asked him several questions and then shared his point of view. He thought Vin should seriously consider the benefits of being able to get noticed quickly in a small law firm like Lesnik, Amoscato versus the struggle that many young lawyers face making an impression at larger firms.

After listening to his son talk for some time about the two firms, Vin's father took a different approach.

"Mio figlio (my son)," John began. "You are in a circumstance that you did not create. You were told to report to duty, and then Eisenhower cut the budget. So you were left scrambling to find a job. Okay, it happened. It's over. But now you should have a choice of places to work. So wipe the slate clean. I'm not telling you what choice to make, but you deserve to choose whichever firm you really want."

Vin immediately let Phil Gordon know that he wouldn't be coming back to the office and went to work for Lum, Farlie & Foster.

About to head into what he hoped was a promising legal career, Vin made a promise to himself—that he would not make work the center of his life, like his father had, but rather use it as a means to enjoy life. Growing up, Vin had only ever taken one vacation with his parents, a rare week off that was spent in Culver's Lake, New Jersey—a trip that my father will quickly tell you was "not very memorable, to say the least. Let's just say it wasn't a Harper's destination." John worked so hard and so often that he had never mastered the skills of relaxing and having a good time. These were skills his son would develop in spades, coupled in time with the desire and financial ability to do so in a host of spectacular venues around the world.

With job in hand, Vin was feeling pretty good about the future. He was finally free from the constraints of the tavern and the worry that his Italian heritage would block him from his career aspirations altogether. He was ready to live life to the fullest.

Looking back on that time, my father tells me, "Here I am. I graduated from law school. I'm studying for the Bar. I don't have any romantic involvement. I'm saying, 'Man, when I become a lawyer, I'm going to be the gay blade around town. I'm going to go every place.' No attachments, you know? Then I meet your mother. Boom—that was it. It was all over." Smiling widely, "Unbelievable..."

Vin as a child with his mother, Mildred

John and Mildred

Young Vincent

Sandy circa 1943
42

Sandy with her parents, Anne and Oscar

Vin in his twenties

From Sandy's modeling portfolio

Vin and Bill Gimello parking cars at the Jersey Shore

*The Budweiser clydesdales in front of John's Tavern, 1951.
John is sitting atop the carriage (in white).*

CHAPTER SIX

Courting

Following on the heels of their first date, Vin and Sandy went out together as many evenings as they could. They frequented many fine local restaurants, their favorite being Mayfair Farms in West Orange. They often followed dinner with a drink at The Moresque, a restaurant and nightclub just around the corner. There was always a piano player or small band at the ready and they would step with ease onto the dance floor, savoring every moment of embrace while floating above the floor. On occasion, Vin would travel into New York City to pick Sandy up from work. Meeting in the garment district, models were "plentiful." My father says, "I used to think my head was on a turnstile to take it all in. But none outshown my love."

Soon into their courtship, Lent approached—that forty-day season when good Catholics give up something they would otherwise miss. While not a serious smoker, by any means, Sandy announced that she was going to give up cigarettes for Lent. Vin thought that was an excellent idea and then, as an interesting marker of how quickly their romance had escalated, casually

47

mentioned that he "would never marry a woman that smoked." Sandy never touched a cigarette again.

Vin was deeply impressed every time he picked Sandy up or dropped her off at home. She was always very respectful to her own parents, whether she was helping decorate the house for special occasions or simply kissing them goodnight for the evening. It was clear that Sandy had a very close relationship with her parents, her father in particular.

Sandy's father, Oscar Yeager, was quite different from Vin's own father. He was a burly man, a former boxer who worked for the Iron Worker's Union in Newark his whole life. He put his muscles into the renovation of a dilapidated house in Oxford on a hundred-acre plot he had bought as a weekend retreat, and filled the fireplace with wood from trees he cut down himself. He would eat a poison oak leaf every spring, believing it would vaccinate him against the perils of the woods.

Oscar raised his daughter and son on the principle of trust. Kids can't be kept in check, he believed, by building walls around them to stop them from performing certain acts. He believed that a good parent should heap trust on their child and make very clear that the worst thing a child could do was break that trust. One night when she was in high school, Sandy silently pushed her father's car down the driveway to go out after curfew with her friends. The next morning, all Sandy's father had to do to drive his point home was ask her, with disappointment in his eyes, if she had taken out the car without his permission. She never broke her curfew again, and the lesson stuck with her deep into her own child-rearing years.

I remember my grandfather as a happy man who would sit me on his lap and discuss the finer aspects of the boilermaker, a drink made (in the UK tradition) by dropping a shot of whisky into a full beer. On my own visits to the house in Oxford that they called the Mountain House, I vividly remember my anticipation at the gift I would receive from him each time. He had a container full of plastic backscratchers, and I was always allowed to pick out whatever shape and color I wanted. A highly practical man, he thought a backscratcher a very handy tool that no one should be caught without.

Not that Oscar Yeager didn't have some faults of his own. His greatest was likely his unwillingness to accept his son Tom's love of opera over football and desire to join the drama club over the baseball team. This mountain man had ideas about what a man should be like, and Tom was not it. It is unclear whether this was made more or less frustrating for Oscar based on the fact that Tom was not actually his biological son, but his nephew. Tom's mother had died in childbirth, and my grandparents agreed to lessen the burden on their brother-in-law, who already had multiple children to raise on his own, and agreed to raise young Tom. Believing all his life that his biological siblings were his cousins, Tom was never told the truth until he was setting off to the submarines of WWII, likely the worst time to tell an already insecure boy earth-shaking news.

I don't have many strong memories about my grandmother, Anne Yeager, save visiting her in the hospital as she was dying from a combination of lung and bone cancer. A troubled woman with a long history of alcoholism, she brought some horrific moments into Sandy's childhood. There were many nights when Oscar would get a phone call from a local bar at 2:00 a.m. letting him know he had to come get his wife, or, worse, nights when there was no phone call and he had to search for her. On several occasions, Sandy went with her father, scanning the streets for her mother, cringing with embarrassment when they finally did. Although Anne had her drinking well under control

49

before my time, my mother's affection always leaned toward her father, which I felt even as a very young child.

But the pair did not seem to disagree when it came to the happiness of their daughter and their grandchild. They both adored Barbara. Oscar called her his "little angel," and they could see that Vin would make a wonderful and loving addition to the family. They were nothing but delighted to see Sandy find real happiness with a promising young man who clearly loved their daughter. And they had always trusted and supported her own life decisions.

Vin would regularly be invited up to the Mountain House. He would help around the house, up on ladders cleaning gutters or helping to fill the Olympic-sized fresh-water pool that Sandy's father had built himself. On one visit, the canvas cot Vin slept on in the screened-in porch suddenly ripped in the middle of the night, spilling him flat on the floor. As much as the embarrassed young suitor tried to downplay the event, they all had a good laugh about it in the morning.

The couple would include Barbara in their dates when possible. One weekend, they headed out to visit Sandy's modeling friend Timmi Ritchie and her husband, Ed, at their house on Long Island. They thought it might be a nice idea to bring a small gift to Peter Ritchie, who was just about Barbara's age, so they brought two balloons with them, one for each of the children. Part way there, one of the balloons burst. Barbara quickly announced, "Oops! There goes Peter's balloon!"

Summertime also included a visit with Timmi and Ed Ritchie to Belmar on the Jersey Shore. Along with them were Tony Ambrose, a fellow law clerk, and a model friend of Timmi and Sandy, whom the girls had arranged to come along as Tony's date. There is a fabulous photo of my parents from that weekend, Sandy holding the hand of the arm draped over her shoulders, sitting so close and so comfortably. She is in a shimmering party dress that looks like it is covered in silk confetti, the perfect match for Vin's tan summer suit. Their eyes are both crystal clear and happy.

Late in July of 1954, Vin and his friend Al set off on a prearranged cruise to Bermuda to celebrate completing June's New Jersey State Bar Exam. Hopeful of good results, the two thought a little R&R and a chance to explore Bermuda was a fitting way to celebrate. Sandy came to the docks with a friend for the bon voyage. She sent Vin off with a few La Coste shirts, one of David Crystal's exclusive offerings. She coyly told him he would surely be turning heads in Bermuda in his new fashionable garb.

Vin wrote two letters to "My Darling Sandy" while he was away, clearly pining for her company.

> *My thoughts throughout our boat trip were of you. As we left the dock and thereafter there was a <u>tremendous</u> yearning to be together. Your companionship would make the entire trip complete. Without it, there is a hollow feeling. There is no doubt in my mind that the feeling was reciprocal on the day we sailed. You see, we're both tuned in on a frequency which only exists where there is present a real depth of feeling. The reception is fine. Enough said?*

And to leave no doubt that his eyes were only for her, he ends his second letter: *P.S. Contrary to my highest expectations, the La Coste shirts don't do a thing for me.*

In September of 1954, much-anticipated news arrived. Vin had passed the NJ State Bar Exam! Sandy and Vin went to their favorite restaurant, Mayfair Farms, to celebrate. Vin was on top of the world. All his work had finally paid off. He was officially a lawyer and no one could stop him now.

It was at dinner that Sandy presented Vin with her first serious gift to him, a beautiful brown alligator skin bill portfolio for him to carry in the inside pocket of his suit jacket. This became a bit of a signature for my father, always carrying in it his business cards, checks, a printed page with important phone numbers, and a recent printout of his calendar. He would carry his credit cards and license in a separate small leather card holder, and his dollar bills in a money clip. Only when I started to see men regularly pulling "wallets" out of their back pockets that looked mistakenly folded up and overstuffed did I realize theirs was the more common option. My mother replaced this leather billfold when the edges were frayed or the leather worn too thin only a handful of times throughout the years, and my father never used anything else.

As usual, after dinner, they went to The Moresque to enjoy the music, and kicked up their heels with a group of revelers that seemed to catch the spark of enthusiasm from the young couple. Vin and Sandy found themselves sipping sparkling burgundy until 2:00 a.m. and buying drinks for anyone who was still there. One such gentleman was Bill English, out for the evening with his wife. Bill was about sixty years old at the time, in senior management at Becton Dickinson, a large pharmaceutical company, and the foursome took to each other right away. After closing the club, they found a diner for breakfast, and before the night was out, Bill English invited Vin and Sandy to join them at the Franklin Lakes Country Club the next day.

Vin had never been inside the walls of an exclusive country club in New Jersey before, and was quite impressed by their surroundings and the hospitality of their host. But it was a story that Bill English told them that stuck with him. Bill began his career at Becton Dickinson as a salesman and within a few months had decided that he was more qualified than his boss for his boss' job. He was quite frustrated by the amount of time it was apparent it would take to gain that position. Years later, after finally succeeding his boss, he made an important discovery. He realized that he couldn't have possibly handled the job when he was first starting out. The job was much more demanding than it seemed to be from below.

Vin found it interesting that this man he had just met would share this story with him. It seems that Bill English saw more than a little bit of himself in his new young lawyer friend and was hoping to inject a smidgen of experience and patience into the young go-getter's swagger.

Patience was not one of my father's given virtues, however. He intended to do great things in his legal career. He also instinctively knew that his professional career would mean nothing without Sandy in his life. Yet he could not reconcile living with such vehement disapproval by his father. He was determined to find a solution to the problem.

CHAPTER SEVEN

The Church

The answer, as far as Vin was concerned, was figuring out how to break through the wall of obstinacy his father had constructed, which only grew stronger with emotional mortar after every argument. His father would not listen to reason, would not consent to meet Sandy, and would not entertain the slightest notion that there might be an alternate way to think about the situation. Vin needed help from an outsider, a reasonable voice that could be trusted and could show his father the way around his own misconceptions.

Growing up, attending Sunday mass was as required as piano practice for Vin. His parents rarely attended church, which is quite ironic considering that the Church was often invoked in the frequent tirades set off by any mention of Vin and Sandy's desired union. But for a young Italian-American boy, mass was required. Every Sunday morning, Vin was given a nickel for the Church and sent off to St. Joseph's from Grand Avenue with all his cousins and Johnny, the eldest, firmly in charge. At offering time, the priest would come to each pew with a wicker basket suspended on a long pole to collect from his parishioners. Frequently, Vin only had two or three pennies to drop into the basket, having given in to the temptations of the candy store on the way. Whenever the priest saw only a few copper coins drop from a boy's hands into his coffer, he readily deciphered the reason, and would give that boy a whack on the back of the head with the basket when collecting from the row behind.

When it came time to attend catechism with his two younger cousins, Gene and Lou, to prepare for confirmation, Vin quickly determined that rote memorization was the best way to avoid the wrath of the nuns, who would send anyone with a wrong answer to a stool in the corner, dunce cap and all. "We didn't learn anything. We just memorized," he says now. After weeks of dutifully attending catechism every Sunday after church and every week day after school, it was announced that the bishop required to oversee confirmation would not be coming to Saint Joseph's that year, and all confirmations would have to be delayed by a year. Determined not to repeat the whole process the following year, Vin decided to lobby Blessed Sacrament, the Irish church in the neighborhood where the bishop would be coming that year to oversee confirmation, to allow the three cousins to receive their confirmation there. The Blessed Sacrament priest was skeptical.

"It takes months of study to be confirmed here at Blessed Sacrament. We require that you really know your cathecism."

"Father," replied Vin, the spokesman for the group, "we have been studying very hard. Ask us anything."

After quizzing the three cousins relentlessly, the priest ultimately agreed that they could all receive their confirmation at the Irish church.

Needless to say, by the time he moved to Market Street, Vin had formed some strong opinions about the Catholic Church.

And while he did get involved in the Church Youth Organization of the new neighborhood church, Mount Carmel, and played on the church baseball team, without his cousin Johnny to watch over him on Sunday mornings, Vin rarely actually made it to church. Instead, after leaving his parents' apartment, he would wander up to Broad Street, looking in the windows of Kresge's Department Store or Bambergers, waiting the appropriate amount of time before returning home. "I figured I didn't need all that noise," he says now.

There was one group of clergy, however, that had made a positive impression on Vin. He found the Franciscan monks who would come and present the Novenas during the celebration of the Feast of St. Francis to be very articulate. They presented themselves as accessible, humble, and merciful, and Vin considered them the most impressive speakers he had ever heard. A famous Alexander Pope quote summed up for Vin his overarching impression of the monks: "To err is human, to forgive divine." Vin needed an outsider to introduce this very notion to his father to settle their family row. After all, Sandy had erred once in marriage, but should clearly be forgiven. She had not even married in a church, so the Church would recognize another marriage. She should be forgiven her past and embraced moving forward. Surely a man of the Franciscan order would see this and help settle the argument once and for all.

Vin called the Franciscan monastery and asked if one of the monks could come to his parents' house for an evening conversation. Feeling quite cunning, he gave his parents no choice in the matter, alerting them during dinner that a visitor was coming later that evening for an important discussion.

When the doorbell rang, Vin sprang up to answer the door with a mixture of anxiety and excitement. He had never met this particular monk before, but he was confident that after both sides of the story were told and this wise brother shared his thoughts on mercy and forgiveness, his parents would have no choice but to embrace their son's wishes. "Frankly," my father says, "I thought I had a stacked deck."

Walking the monk into the living room, Vin outlined the situation and his hopes for gaining the good brother's input to help them resolve their disagreement. The brother introduced himself, sharing a bit of his background as a former real estate agent who joined the order at the age of thirty-nine. Suddenly Vin began to worry that this man in the brown robe was perhaps less than the vaulted figure he had envisioned. How deeply had this man adopted the Franciscan ways and philosophies? Was he yet wise enough to take the long view on an issue such as the one being put before him?

Vin shared his love for Sandy and his reasoning behind why a marriage between them should be blessed by the Church and cause no consternation for his family. He then listened to his father articulate once again his forceful disapproval. When the monk shared his thoughts, he did not characterize the situation as a "very difficult one which should take careful consideration," as Vin had assumed, or even suggest that it would be wise to "pause and ask each party to be open-minded about the alternate views expressed by the other," as Vin had considered the lowest bar a reasonable man would suggest. Instead, the monk in no uncertain terms was clear that "the family would be adversely affected" if Vin were to wed Sandy and that Vin's desire to do this "was not in the interest of the family unit." Vin was dumbfounded. Not only did the walls of his father's resistance not come crumbling down that night, they became ever more buttressed by the monk's conviction.

John did see, however, that his son had not been swayed in the least by the words of the monk, writing him off as an unknown entity he should not have brought into the conversation (at least not without being deposed beforehand, the young barrister realized). And John was as desperate as his son to have the argument resolved. So he decided to take a page out of his son's own playbook, this time with someone whom John believed Vin would listen to.

Father Fuino was a good-looking young priest at Mount Carmel who knew Vin because of his involvement in the CYO and the church baseball team in high school. Another meeting was arranged, this time by John. Vin was extremely hesitant. Father Fuino wore the dark robes of a priest, not the humble brown coverings of the monks. Worse, Father Fuino was of Italian descent. He understood well the mores of families with strong Italian roots, and therefore might have a natural bias akin to his father's. But given the surprise meeting Vin had organized with the monk, he was in no position to refuse this one.

Once again, both sides stated their case, and, once again, Vin was "shot down." As he says, "At this point there was some question about my persuasive abilities as a budding lawyer. Fortunately, they improved over time, but at this point they were inadequate." Worse, with two members of the Church now supporting his father's way of thinking, Vin had grave concerns that this fissure could ever be solved. His parents were forcing him to make a choice: forsake the love of his life, or separate himself forever from his family.

When Vin told Sandy about these two conversations, she was "beyond appalled." A practicing Catholic educated in Catholic school, Sandy was the most devoted Catholic in the bunch, and was shocked that the reaction of the clergy was so strong and so one-sided. This was not her experience with the Church, and she was sorely hurt and disappointed that they would advocate against a pairing based on love. Even worse that they would judge her so severely without knowing her.

With pressure mounting from all sides, Vin could no longer abide the tension at home. To his parents' extreme dismay, he packed up his things and moved out. The little white pill surely came out once again, but Vin had already closed the door behind him.

While Sandy was relieved to see Vin finally take a strong stand in support of their relationship, she was equally heartbroken for him. She understood how painful walking out that door must have been for him. Sons should not ever have to shut out their fathers. And fathers should certainly not shut out their sons. Clearly, a woman was going to have to step in and fix this. Without telling Vin, she decided to go see Father Fuino herself.

CHAPTER EIGHT

Sandy

Being sick enough to stay home from school was an infrequent yet cherished privilege in our house. One winter morning, the shards that dug into the sides of my neck every time I swallowed made me pitch forward and raise my chin a bit to help the saliva find its course without enraging the fire inside my throat. Between swallows, I was nestled into my parents' bed, surrounded by the pillows on my mother's side, waiting for the penicillin to take hold. The green and yellow flowery print on the bedspread, headboard, and bedskirt matched the two chairs placed perfectly beside the bay window. Through the window I could see the brick patio and the two pine trees that would faithfully hold our hammock as soon as the weather graced the New Jersey suburbs with the warmth of spring. By this time we were living in Short Hills, yet another step in my parents' westward march away from Newark.

The white wicker tray settled on my lap was my command central for the duration of my recovery. This was the only kind of day when I was allowed to watch TV with abandon. The wicker pocket on the right side of my tray held the TV remote, not something, as the youngest of five, I was ever given license to operate or permission to indulge in on a regular day. To my left, on my mother's nightstand, sat a brass bell in the shape of a woman wearing a bonnet and a multi-layered petticoat, a Southern belle from another era. I knew I could ring her at any time to ask for anything. I don't remember ever ringing her for attention as much as I remember loving her for knowing that anything I truly needed was never more than a shake of the wrist away. Just before the mid-day rumble began to make itself heard in my stomach, my mother was there, asking what I might like for lunch. The cold Jell-o then magically appeared, coupled with a suggestion that the warm soup first might also help soothe my throat, and, of course, that another gargle with warm salt water after I had finished was important.

Just as I was feeling that I had beat this particular bug in record time, my mother swept through the room, lowering the shades on the windows, taking the remote from my hands and the tray from my lap, and told me that it was time for a nap. After hearing me declare that I was really feeling good and didn't need to sleep, she fluffed my pillows, brushed the hair from my forehead, and said, "Trust me, sweetheart, you need to rest." As she aimed the remote at the TV to take the last bit of direct light from the room, I continued my plea.

"But, Mom, I love Greg Brady with curly hair. Can I just watch this one episode?"

She hesitated a moment so as not to douse the light from her next thought. She turned and looked at me quite intently and narrowed her gaze, raising one eyebrow a bit and closing slightly the space around her light blue eyes to put emphasis on her response.

"Don't be too impressed by movie stars. They are rarely what they seem."

And with that, the TV went dark.

Two hours later, I woke from a luxurious sleep, noticing that my legs felt stronger when I got up to repeat the salt-water gargle. No more than one day of homework needed to be rescued from my classmates, and I was back on the path.

I hadn't given much thought to my mother's comments on stardom—after all, no one in my family is short on opinions—until I was rooting around the attic space behind my sister's bedroom one day. This space was my indoor treehouse, my hidden playground, and where my make-believe was sometimes derailed by suddenly noticing the edge of a small canvas stacked between book spines or seeing the top of a filing box askew. In the middle of my solo game of "office manager," which put me in charge of supplies and incoming appointments, I stumbled upon a small stack of black-and-white photographs. One photograph pictured my mother with Bob Hope, the only stranger I recognized among the many unfamiliar faces. One of the biggest stars in the world in the 1940s and 1950s, his star power had diminished so little by the 1970s that I knew exactly who he was. When I asked her about the photograph, she temporarily lapsed into a brief memory that included something about flying on a private plane to Las Vegas. Seeing my eyes open a bit wider, craving the next detail, she caught herself.

"Don't be impressed. What sounds glamorous is often anything but."

Waving away the thought, she turned back to the meatballs that were simmering on the stove and added another bay leaf to the pot. With that, she treated the photo as if it were as frivolous as a childhood escapade caught on film with someone you haven't seen since the third grade, and dismissed it. So did I.

I didn't press further into the past until I stumbled upon my parents' wedding photographs. These pictures were not arranged in an album proudly perched on a coffee table for perusal by dinner party guests, but hidden amongst the slew of faux-veneer brown filing boxes in that attic playground. The first thing I noticed was that there was almost no one at the wedding. The next thing I noticed was that my oldest sister, Barbara, was in the photographs.

Rushing to find my mother, I went immediately into the kitchen. She was at the sink, washing snap peas, carefully pulling the gnarling strings from the pods.

"Mom! Barbara is in your wedding photos! How is that possible?"

Barbara was always there in my life without ever really being there. She went off to college two months before I was born, which meant that we never lived in the same house together. I was the youngest by a wide margin. My family was complete before I got there. I never compared my parents' wedding anniversary to Barbara's age to notice the discrepancy, and if my older siblings had done the math, no one had ever bothered to share this little tidbit of information with me. The one calculation that was obvious to me for as long as I could count was that Barbara was nine years older than my brother John. When I had asked my mother about this odd spacing of children, she had not hesitated to share that she had had two miscarriages after Barbara, both boys. After soothingly answering a few of the naïve questions that jolted into my mind about what having a miscarriage means, I had tucked my mother's answers into my safe pocket of truths about the world.

Hearing my outburst as I came barreling into the kitchen, my mother raised her gaze from the snap peas to the greenhouse outside the window over the sink, and remained with her back

64

to me long enough for my next two or three gasping breaths to move into a more natural rhythm. Turning around, she wiped her hands on a dishtowel and leaned against the counter. Her answer came in a very steady voice, one that did not suggest her usual calm as much as it suggested a push to get through the sentence without betraying emotion. She told me that she had been married once before, when she lived in California, and had had Barbara while in her first marriage. She then quickly moved to the more important matter in her eyes.

"Your father adopted Barbara years ago, and so he is her father and she is your sister."

My curiosity was not in the least bit satiated and I sorted through the fourteen or fifteen questions I had in my head to try to make sense of this new information. Whichever question I chose, my mother managed to put a lifetime of silence between me and any answers by simply saying, "It is a time in my life that I prefer to forget. In fact, I mostly pretend it didn't happen at all. Now, since you are downstairs, could you please set the table for me?"

That was it. End of discussion.

My initial desire to know more was immediately squelched by a thin layer of fear. What could have been so unspeakable that she had to forget altogether? And how could anything terrible have happened to her? This was the woman who ran our household with control so elegant you weren't always entirely sure who was in charge. She would secretly turn off the alarm my father set to catch my older brothers missing curfew. If I didn't get out of bed within five minutes of her wakeup call to me on the intercom that was built into the old office phones we used at home, she would buzz back knowingly, telling me to put both feet on the floor. She single-handedly orchestrated gourmet dinners for us six nights a week, but had us all equally appreciative of the cooking-free Sunday ritual of Entenmann's Crumb Coffee Cake for breakfast, Millburn Deli Sloppy Joes for lunch, and pizza with *60 Minutes* for dinner. She wrote notes to school in penmanship I wondered if I would ever master as a grown-up, ran every school organization that ever asked her, and could back up the U-Haul attached to the station wagon for our annual summer journeys to Cape Cod with the serpentine accuracy of a trained truck driver. Most importantly, I had always been able to go to my mother about anything bothering me, and she would validate my feelings and quell my fears with a tenderness I knew nowhere else. Whatever had created cold silence in my warm touchstone, I wanted no part of. And so I dropped it, almost holding my breath as I wished away the eerie stillness in the room.

Small pieces of information from her California years would inch out occasionally, though sparingly. I remember one evening sitting in my mother's dressing room watching her get ready for a night out with my father. I loved to watch her at her makeup desk, the top of her robe crisscrossed below her collar-bone and sparkling diamond necklace. Stockings and high heels already on, she would blow dry her hair, saying she wished it were as thick as mine, and wisp mascara onto her lashes, telling me I was lucky to have such dark lashes that would never need mascara. When I admired a set of gold and sapphire starburst earrings in her open jewelry box, she told me that they had been given to her along with a matching ring by a roommate in California. The set had been a gift from Cary Grant, but this roommate had inexplicably given them to my mother. She, in turn, later gave the ring to Barbara. Contrary to my mother's earlier pronouncement about movie stars, those earrings took on a new luster for me.

I also remember the first time I noticed an illustration in a small bedroom in our Cape house that looked like a shadow of Mickey Mouse swinging a lasso. I found it a bit menacing, not the happy illustration of Mickey Mouse I had grown accustomed to, and so I assigned it no particular value. It wasn't until much later that I understood it had been personally given to my mother by Walt Disney, signed as a gift to Barbara.

Halloween of my sophomore year of high school brought another opening in the door to the West. My mother's sewing prowess did not stop at making her own clothes in her modeling days. I thought all kids had a built-in tailor in their house to hem or alter any item needed. But this was simple stuff compared to her costumes, first winning countless prizes with my father at costume parties, and then creating an inventory of Halloween garb for us kids that made the annual even a rite of passage—whose turn was it to wear the tiger costume and who was getting stuck with the geisha girl outfit? (My brothers were not exempt.) Did you fit in the matador this year, or would this be your year to be the golden lion?

Having grown out of the line-up by high school, and with a big on-stage Halloween parade coming up at school, Mom took me into the closet on the second-story landing of our Beechcroft Street house, full of clothes she had long since exiled from her wardrobe. Sorting through the many hangers, most draped with long plastic covers, pulling the edge up on a few, lingering on some others, she found what she was looking for and suggested that I should consider being a cowgirl. She pulled out a light blue wool skirt and matching top with silver buttons. There was dark blue suede fringe all along the bottom of the skirt, down the sides of both arms, and along the chest of the jacket. I loved it on sight. When I grabbed my Colorado cowboy hat and a bottle of shampoo to complete my look as "The Flex Girl," my mother laughed and said that her old friends Roy Rogers and Dale Evans would appreciate the look.

"You knew Roy Rogers?"

I had proudly brought home my Roy Roger's Restaurant Membership Card years earlier after an outing with my best friend, Molly, with no comment from my mother whatsoever. Her choice to remember was always unpredictable.

"Sure," she said. "I knew him and Dale very well. We had a lot of fun together. But that was a long time ago."

After giving me a gaze that said she approved of my outfit for the catwalk at school, she waved me toward her.

"Now let me pin the side of that skirt for you. I think I need to take it in just a bit."

My mind silently spun. I recalled the photo of Bob Hope that I had written off as a chance encounter. And then the Cary Grant jewelry, which she had treated as no more unusual than roommates swapping sweaters. Had my mother gotten a real turn in that starry world? And if she had gotten a true taste of that kind of glamour and excitement, what kind of interior switch had she flipped to abandon all that for her role as selfless caretaker of our little world?

Then the old fear rose anew. How many people have truly star-studded experiences and don't talk about them with relish? What had actually happened during those years to warrant putting so much distance between her homemaker self and that time? I was too afraid to ask.

She turned me again and marked the new spot for the button with a pin.

Sandy graduated from Our Lady of Good Counsel in Newark, New Jersey, in 1944. She went to work as a receptionist for an office building in Newark, but it wasn't long before she was persuaded to give modeling school a chance. Apparently she was a natural and was soon employed by Henri Bendel's in New York City as a runway model.

In the fall of 1946, the Navy sponsored a "Navy Queen" contest one month before their annual Navy Day celebration, looking for a young lady with "beauty and brains" to add some elegance to the face of the Navy and to create some good PR to help with recruiting. Sandy won, and with the honor came many prizes, the most coveted a new black-and-white TV (her father marveled at the ability to have his friends over to his own house to watch the latest prize fight instead of having to gather down at the local pub). She was given limousine and airplane rides to many appearances. The person she remembered the most from that time was the sweet older man who drove her limousine. He worried over her and told her to "watch out for the wolves."

Sometime in 1947, Sandy landed a modeling job with Adrian's of California in Beverly Hills and set off for adventure. Hollywood in 1947 was a sparkling time. Despite the repeated attempts of the government to hunt down "communists" among the ever-more influential silver screeners, the golden years of Hollywood were in full swing. The top twenty grossing films in 1947 included performances from such legendary names as Gary Cooper, Cary Grant, Myrna Loy, Betty Grable, Bing Crosby, Bob Hope, Humphrey Bogart, Lauren Bacall, and Rita Hayworth. Spencer Tracy and Katharine Hepburn were already an item, and Marilyn Monroe made her first screen appearance that year in the uncredited role of a phone operator in *The Shocking Miss Pilgrim.* Frank Sinatra's popularity had already soared and declined with the bobby-soxer crowd, soon to be reinvigorated by his starring role with Gene Kelly in *Take Me out to the Ball Game* two years later.

The ability of television to create stars right in people's living rooms was beginning in earnest. The World Series was broadcast for the first time in 1947, with the newly signed Jackie Robinson and the Brooklyn Dodgers facing off against the New York Yankees (the Yankees won four games to three, I'm sorry to say). Harry S. Truman delivered the first live presidential address on the small screen that year, and *The Howdy-Doody Show, Kukla, Fran and Ollie,* and *Meet the Press* all debuted on the fourteen thousand or so TVs across the country.

And in 1947, Roy Rogers was a full-fledged Western matinee idol. He had made over 70 movies, and was one of the original symbols of the American Western cowboy, riding his horse Trigger and crooning about the vast frontier.

By 1948, Roy Roger's contract with his back-up band, the Sons of the Pioneers, had run its course, and he decided to hire a new band, The Riders of the Purple Sage. The band was fronted by a singer-songwriter named Foy Willing, who at that time had recorded over twenty singles, appeared in twelve movies, and had performed in radio broadcasts for the American troops alongside such luminaries as Lena Horne, Bob Hope, Ozzie and Harriet, and Danny Thomas. Backing up Roy Rogers, the Riders would appear in thirteen movies and perform on a weekly radio broadcast called "The Roy Rogers Show" every Sunday night for three years. In 1947, Foy Willing was walking into the height of his career.

Sandy somehow fell into good company upon arrival in Hollywood. She roomed with Betty Hensel, a former model who was dating Cary Grant. An article in the Binghamton Press from 1947 shows a photo of Betty and Cary together with a quote stating that they are really just "very good friends" even though she "wears his ring," apparently the same ring she later gave to Sandy.

None of us know how Sandy and Foy Willing met or what kindled their relationship, but they were married in August of 1948 in Las Vegas, and Barbara was born in September of 1949.

All I know about Foy I garnered from a book written by his third wife, Sharon Lee Willing, called *No One to Cry to, A Long Hard Ride into the Sunset with Foy Willing and The Riders of the Purple Sage.* Sandy was Foy's second wife. Foy had two children from his first marriage, twins Glenn and Anne, born in 1939, and while he stayed close friends with both his first wife and his third, he was unable to maintain any of his marriages in the traditional sense. Sharon never divorced him, but she left him two years after they were married, and they did not live together for the last ten years of his life. He was clearly a troubled man who struggled mightily with alcohol and drugs. Sharon Willing states in her book, "At what point in his life Foy's social drinking became problematic for him, I doubt even he could tell us today, but it was to have an impact on his career—and his personal relationships—that would have more far-reaching consequences than he could have possibly foretold."

One of his worst spells seems to have been when he was married to Sandy. "By 1951, all the freewheeling and partying might have caught up with Foy. The story that circulated about why The Riders left Republic [their recording company] was not flattering to Foy. Rumor had it that he was drinking so heavily that he could not stay on a horse." Sharon also states that "the year 1951 was spent touring around San Francisco, Salt Lake, Palm Springs, and venues around Los Angeles." In 1952, with the public's interest in Westerns waning, Foy disbanded The New Riders and "he left Los Angeles to manage an NBC radio station in Sacramento." Foy's son Glenn states in the book that he and his mother went to San Jose in 1953 to "check on Foy, who was by then playing in a small bar" and that he "was not in

71

good shape." These few pieces of the puzzle would suggest that between 1951 and 1953, Foy was mostly if not entirely an absentee husband.

What was that time like for Sandy? Did she ever try to cover for his drinking binges, ashamed by needing to apologize to friends like Roy and Dale when Foy would slip up? Were his long absences voluntary? Had he willingly abandoned his new young family in favor of the freedom of partying on the road? Or had Sandy thrown him out, horrified by his drunken behavior and the impact it might have on their young daughter? Whatever transpired exactly through that time period, it was enough to entirely disillusion Sandy with the idea of Hollywood. Much more importantly, it was enough to steel her courage to leave her husband and file for divorce on the grounds of "mental cruelty." Sandy filed for divorce in May of 1953 and left California within the year. The divorce became final in May of 1955. She told Foy that she would never talk to Barbara about him. And so while Foy technically had visitation rights and was expected to pay one hundred dollars per month for child support, neither ever occurred, and Sandy and Barbara never saw Foy again.

By early 1955, while waiting for her divorce to be finalized, Sandy was embroiled in another heart-rending situation. Unsure whether Vin's parents would ever accept her as a part of his life, she knew their future together might rely on a terrible choice for Vin. Moving out was hard enough on him. Cutting ties completely was not a choice she wanted the man she loved to have to make. She was equally determined to make good use of the courage she had summoned in California. She was not prepared to let three men who had never even met her put up an insurmountable blockade between her and the chance of a happy family life with a man she loved and respected. This had to be set right, and she knew that she was the one to do it.

CHAPTER NINE

Confrontation

Surveying herself in the mirror, confirming that she had chosen the right suit for her meeting with Father Fuino, I can only imagine what Sandy was wearing and what she was feeling that day. She was a devout Catholic, and had faith that a sincere conversation with Father Fuino would convince him that he had been badly mistaken in the advice he had given to Vin's family. She was clearly worthy of the family, deeply in love with Vin, and there should be no remaining questions for the father after their meeting.

I can see her walking up the stairs of Mount Carmel, steadying her breath, smoothing any possible wrinkles out of her skirt, and remembering her small and graceful runway steps, even though her determination would naturally cause her to walk much more forcefully down the aisle of the church.

Seated in a pew with Father Fuino, Sandy tells him her story, emphasizing her devotion to the Church, her desire to give her daughter a stable and happy family life, and the deep love shared between her and Vin. Surely the father could see that love like this should not be discouraged. It should be embraced and celebrated.

Father Fuino was quite taken by this elegant woman. Sandy could tell watching his face and his eyes while she was talking that he was affected by her warmth and sincerity. He was hanging on her words, and her confidence grew. Just as she suspected, it would take the reason and grace of a woman to turn this situation around. She was at the precipice of tipping the first domino in favor of her future union with Vin.

Once Sandy came to the end of her plea, I can see Father Fuino moving in a bit closer to her, his body language showing that she had successfully transformed herself in his eyes from a faceless character in a family dispute to a sympathetic and graceful woman who deserved his attention. He reached out to her hand, a comforting gesture that better represented her experience with the Church than the nonsense Vin had spoken of.

But Father Fuino's hand did not pat hers, as was her expectation. It lingered there. When she looked up into his eyes, his held hers. When she looked back down at his hand, he was slowly moving it up her arm.

Ripping her hand away, she quickly stood up in disbelief. The ground seemed to shift a bit under her feet, her stomach suddenly nauseous. She placed her hand on the pew to steady herself, keeping her glare directed toward him for long enough to register her outrage. I will never know if she told Father Fuino what she thought of him just then, or if her disgust was made clear by the turn of her back and the echoes of her high heels as she stormed back down the aisle, her steps not quite as measured as they had been on the way in.

Knowing nothing about Sandy's meeting with Father Fuino, Vin was dealing with the outcome of a meeting of his own. Not long after moving out of his parents' house and into a boarding house, Vin received a call from his Uncle Don, inviting him to dinner. He realized immediately that Uncle Don was sent as an ambassador from his parents. They met at a local restaurant and were seated at a booth across from one another. Mildred had chosen her ambassador wisely, knowing that Vin had great respect for her younger brother, not knowing that Vin would eventually name his second son after him. Vin considered Uncle Don to be a man of substance, a fellow musician, by now a colonel and veteran of World War II, and the husband of gorgeous Aunt Grace.

After ordering their food, Uncle Don made the purpose of the dinner clear. Vin's choice to move out of the house had made his parents incredibly distraught. It was "killing his mother." While sympathetic to Vin's situation, Don implored Vin to move back home and work out the disagreement before he destroyed his relationship with his parents forever. Vin's father was not going to be the one to blink first, and perhaps this gesture of reconciliation would push things in the right direction. While moved by Don's concern and deeply disturbed by the level of his mother's distress, Vin did not see how anything would be different. He wanted to be with Sandy, and if he had been unsuccessful in convincing his parents of the validity of their love already, how would moving back in possibly help the situation?

Like a good negotiator who needed to go back to his clients with at least some semblance of a victory, Uncle Don cut Vin a deal.

"Move back in and give it two weeks. I have high hopes that you will all be able to work it out. But if you give it two weeks and you and your parents can't agree, then you do whatever you feel you have to do."

When Don saw Vin hesitate, he used his last card. "Vin, your father has not been feeling well since you left. This is not good for his heart."

Vin did not share his uncle's optimism for a positive outcome, but he was unable to turn him down. In an effort not to disappoint his uncle, he rationalized that two weeks would pass quickly. Having a hard time justifying the move even to himself, however, he decided that unless the tide miraculously turned, there was no reason to trouble Sandy with this latest development. And so he moved back home without telling her.

Later that week, Vin and Sandy were out on another date. Sandy told him of her horrifying experience with Father Fuino. He was infuriated, and this put the darkest mark yet in Vin's inner journal of feelings about the Catholic Church. Sandy was becoming less enamored every day.

Bringing Sandy home after their date, Vin parked his car on Branchbrook Drive in Belleville, just north of Newark. As they walked toward the apartment Sandy and Barbara shared with her parents, the couple commiserated about why their desire to be together had to be met with such resistance. Why couldn't everyone see how strong their love was and support their desire to be together? They wound their way along the cement path cut into the grass lawn, which was shared by several two-story brick apartment buildings. The matching buildings were all divided into four or five separate apartments, each with their own white door, one white-shuttered window on each floor, and a front stoop. The large dogwood tree closest to Sandy's apartment was in full bloom, reminding her of the sunny afternoon she and Vin had just spent with Barbara at nearby Branchbrook Park, enjoying the dozens of dogwoods in all their pink splendor. Anyone in the park that day would have assumed they were young parents out with their adored little girl. And even a casual passerby would have smiled at the love apparent between them. Why wouldn't his parents welcome that sight?

As Sandy opened the door to her parents' apartment and stepped inside, she suddenly realized that she hadn't asked about Vin's new living quarters.

"I got so wrapped up in talking about Father Fuino, I forgot to ask you, Vin." She turned toward him and put her hand on his arm. "How is everything going at the boarding house?"

Vin froze. Looking into Sandy's eyes, he knew he could not lie. Head spinning, he also knew that the truth would make her question everything. His decision to move out of his parents' house had made them accomplices in love. They had found strength in each other, united against a torrent of family history, pre-established beliefs, and a culture that did not leave much room for reconsideration of preconceptions.

Finding it hard to breathe, his blood pressure dropping, he began to feel woozy. The choice to stand together had brought them closer and made them ever more sure of their love for each other. How could he let her doubt his resolve?

At that moment, the unthinkable happened. Vin fainted, landing in a heap on the floor.

After a moment of shock, Sandy's nurturing instincts took over. Gently reviving Vin, she hurried to get him a cold wash cloth and a glass of water. Sitting on the floor with him until he felt better, Sandy wondered at the level of emotion in this man and the incredible toll his parents' disapproval was taking on him. Clearly, his love for his parents and fear of losing them ran deep, and, even still, his love for her was pulling him ever more in her direction. How could they solve this mess?

He let her sympathy eliminate the need to directly answer her question.

CHAPTER TEN

Lost

Later that week, Vin's unflappable secretary, Jeanne Martino, let him know he had a phone call.

"Mr. Apruzzese, Sandy is on the line."

"Hi, San." He rarely used her full name. "How are you, sweetheart?"

There was a lengthy pause.

"San?"

Her voice sounded like she was clutching the receiver. "Vin, I am calling to let you know that I never want to see you again."

"What?" The spring air coming in through the open window in his office felt suddenly stifling. The shaky silence on the other end of the line wasn't helping. "San, what are you talking about?"

"I just came from your parents' house."

His chest felt like it had just tried a thoroughbred's six-foot jump and hit the bars hard.

"Seeing you faint made me so upset the other night. I decided that I had to meet them. I wanted them to know how much we loved each other and how heartbroken I was to see the distress their disapproval was causing you. I had to let them know how terrible I felt about the fact that you had moved out, that your feelings about me had caused you to move out."

Vin sank in his chair. Fluid was rushing through his head. He wasn't sure he was entirely comprehending what he was hearing.

"Imagine how I felt when they told me that you had moved back in."

Silence. Then a brief try, "San... I..."

"No, Vin. I thought I knew where you stood. If you don't have the guts to call the shot and go through with it, then maybe you don't really love me after all."

He didn't know what to say in that moment. He knew there was no excuse he could offer. The fog in his head was making it difficult to imagine how he could repair the damage. And before he could utter another word, the conversation was over.

Vin was like an automaton the rest of the day. If he spoke to clients, he didn't remember the conversation. If he studied a brief, he circled back over the same sections multiple times. By the time he got home, he was completely exhausted, a feeling not warranted by the feeble amount of work he had accomplished that afternoon.

He found his parents in the kitchen, his father sitting on the kitchen counter. One look at their son told them that he knew about Sandy's visit.

"So, you met her."

His father nodded. With anxiety, Mildred saw the argument coming again.

"Oh, Vinny, she looked so lovely in her chiffon dress and that wide-brimmed hat—"

"Mildred!" And off his father went.

As if following a set script for the umpteenth time, the same fight progressed with all the same points, counterpoints, and all the fury. Except now Vin was arguing with a desperation he hadn't quite reached before. And this time, his father's last comment veered off his standard lines.

"I tell you, son, I'll never stand for it. But if you love her as much as you say you do, you're a damn fool if you don't marry her."

Rather than rushing into his next retort, Vin's mouth fell slack. He blinked. For the second time that day, he couldn't believe what he was hearing. His father had budged without budging. He would never give his blessing to the couple, but he understood the choice his son had to make. My father says, "At that instant, I knew in his heart, though he could not bring himself to accept it, that it was my choice that mattered."

Vin walked out of the kitchen, packed his bags, and moved out for the last time.

He called Sandy as soon as he could to apologize and tell her that he had moved out for good, but she would not answer her phone. She would not return any messages. Holding out some hope that her anger would cool with a little time, Vin wrote her a note reminding her that their big weekend in Cherry Hill was coming up. Surely she would still go with him. She knew it was a very important event for him; all of his key clients would be there. They had been to a meeting together there once before, and Vin had been so proud to "show off his new love." They had had a wonderful time and had really been looking forward to going back to enjoy the beautiful facility and the many entertaining events. Most of all, it promised to be a beautiful spring weekend that they could enjoy together. His note went unanswered. He tried calling her again at work. He tried calling her at home. She still would not take his calls, and he began to feel a deep unease.

The weekend at the Cherry Hill Inn came and went in a cloud of dismay for Vin. As counsel to the Building Contractor's Association of New Jersey at the time, he had many clients to entertain, but the big smile and hearty handshake Vin usually offered them were muted and unenthusiastic. The gorgeous weather and impressive facility did nothing for Vin without Sandy there. He left the meeting at one point to get away from the forced socializing and clear his mind. Looking for any distraction to quiet his restless heart and mind, he found himself wandering into Philadelphia, a thirty-minute drive from Cherry Hill, and visiting Scott & Huntsinger, a clothing store from his law school years. Buying a new suit failed to even momentarily reduce his growing anxiety. Sandy's refusal to come to Cherry Hill was a very bad sign and made him believe for the first time that he might have lost her forever.

By the end of the following week, Vin was desperate. He was becoming even less productive at work. With still no word from Sandy, his stomach bothered him so much that he thought he might have ulcers. He could not imagine his life without her. He wanted to dance with her again; he wanted to share all the triumphs and challenges of his career with her. He wanted to hold her hand again. He needed her in his life.

Not knowing what else to do, he finally called Sandy's friend Timmi Ritchie at work.

"Hi Timmi, It's Vin."

She paused for a moment, unsure what to say.

"Hello, Vin." Her voice was measured.

"Listen, Timmi. I can't get Sandy to return any of my phone calls. I have tried for weeks. I have to see her. I was hoping you might be able to help."

He could tell she was carefully considering the situation. Timmi had most certainly gotten an earful from Sandy on the topic and knew full well that she had cut off communication with him. But Timmi had also witnessed the ease they felt around each other, the genuine affection they shared. She knew they had been in love. And with any luck, Sandy was having a hard time hiding her own misery at the current situation.

He filled the silence. "Just tell me where I can find her."

She sighed. "We are doing a show tonight at the Waldorf Astoria in the city. It's for the Standard Brand convention. Grand Ballroom. Sandy will be there."

"Timmi," he was having a hard time steadying his voice. "Do me a favor, will you? Don't tell her I'm there until after the show. But don't let her leave until I get a chance to talk to her."

Timmi paused again. A passive piece of information was quickly turning into an active scheme.

"Please, Timmi," he tried. "I have to see her."

"Okay, Vin. I'll do it. You know the door we usually leave through. I'll make sure she doesn't leave until you are there."

The day passed in a blur of slow motion and unimportant activities. As soon as the clock reported that the day was heading into evening, Vin left his office and set off for New York.

CHAPTER ELEVEN

Declaration

Driving down Park Avenue, Vin lucks into a parking spot not too far from the hotel. A doorman points him to the Grand Ballroom, and he finds a seat in the mezzanine. The lights dim. Anxiously, he watches the David Crystal models come on stage to display the latest line of cruise and sportswear. They come out one by one and take their places on a pyramid, the first four girls along the bottom row. The next three models saunter across the stage and step up to create the second row, slightly higher than the first. He glances at his watch, wondering how long the show will be and whether or not he will get to her in time. Two more models step onto the stage and walk up to the third row, higher still than the last. He is not sure how he will keep his nerves at bay while waiting for the chance to see her again.

And then he sees her, standing on the top of the pyramid. Nine girls below her, she is wearing white shark skin slacks and a summery yellow top and looks stunning. He can't stand the fact that he must share her with the twelve hundred other people in the room, or that she is perched so far away from him on the top of that pyramid.

Timmi has kept her promise. Sandy doesn't know that Vin has come to the David Crystal show to find her. She is executing her performance flawlessly. These events have a bit of the feel of a Broadway show for the models, with several clothing changes and a flurry of designers, make-up artists, and fashion experts fawning over each girl to make sure she is ready to display the next outfit to perfection. Sandy is at ease throughout the chaos, knowing she will be set up to look her best.

As she smiles over the crowd, instantly infusing the stage with warmth, Vin sees the woman who will walk arm-in-arm with their children through the snow-packed streets of Snowmass singing Christmas carols, turn an old garage-sale table into the whimsical centerpiece of their summer dinners, and turn heads walking hand-in-hand with him into countless rooms around the world. He says to himself, "Apruzzese, if you don't marry this girl, you are nuts!" and shakes his head, thinking back on everything that got them to this place, including his own serious mistake. Maybe she was right. Maybe he hadn't had the courage to make the choice his father was forcing him to make. Not until now. She had to know that he was resolved and unwavering in his intention to be with her.

The show seems endless. He had previously enjoyed unfettered opportunities like this to gaze at Sandy, watching her glide about the stage, knowing that he would have her all to himself for a quiet dinner and some dancing afterward. But on this night, the more he feels all eyes in the crowd on her, the more anxious he is. What if she refuses to see him after the show? What will he do then?

Finally, the last model leaves the stage, and Vin is soon wading through the hundreds of business people heading to their next convention activity. He rushes outside to the door he knows the models will be using.

When Sandy walks out of the building, I can picture her being initially torn between her lingering anger and her delight upon seeing him. But refusing to accept phone calls is one thing. Standing in front of him, she has trouble keeping up her guard.

His deep brown eyes meet hers. He is by her side in an instant.

"San..."

His suffering shows in his eyes, mixed with lingering hope and excitement. She does not resist. Vin puts his arm around Sandy and leads her toward his car.

"San, I'm so sorry. I moved out for good. I can't stand being without you."

He can tell by her lean into him that she is drawn into his words, into him. Once they are inside the car, Vin's emotions hit a crescendo.

"San, we're going to get married!" And they are in each other's arms.

I have a Western Union telegram that my father likely sent to my mother a day or two after that night. It was posted from Newark at 12:09 p.m. on May 4, 1955, to Sandy Willing at David Crystal and Co, 498 7th Ave, New York. It reads:

"UOY EVOL I NO MATTER HOW YOU SPELL IT TWIST OR TURN IT, IT STILL MEANS THE SAME: LOVE =VIN="

My father admits now that their engagement was more of a declaration than a proposal, but it clearly did the trick. They left the Waldorf and went to their favorite French bistro on the West Side to celebrate. The couple quickly set the date of July 10 for the wedding and began preparations for their life together.

First they had to find an apartment that would be suitable for their new little family of three and be ready for move-in after the wedding. As luck would have it, just at this time they met Marie and Merritt Viscardi, who owned a two-family home in East Orange. They had two daughters, one the exact same age as Barbara, and were looking for a tenant to rent the second-floor apartment. With one visit to 53 Ampere Parkway, Vin and Sandy decided to rent it. There was a good amount of work that needed to be done to spruce up the place, so Vin scraped together a few sparse items of furniture and immediately moved his things from the boarding house to the new apartment. This way he could lawyer by day and renovate the apartment by night. Vin spent many late nights breaking down walls and painting rooms followed by pizza and beer with Merritt and a few cousins who came to help.

Meanwhile, Sandy set about making dresses for herself and Barbara for the wedding. She made her own out of beautiful white lace, tight at the waist with a bell-shaped skirt that swayed just above her ankles. She designed it with removable sleeves so that she could easily wear it again. My favorite photograph of my parents is from their honeymoon—she is wearing the sleeveless version of that gorgeous dress. Barbara's dress was made of what looks like organza with a short flouncy skirt and a big white satin sash tied at the back. The perfect flower girl.

Vin handled all the plans for the reception. Hosted at Mayfair Farms, it included exactly eight people in addition to the bride and groom: Sandy's parents, the matron of honor, Timmi Ritchie, and her husband, the best man, Tony "Docky" Doganiero, Vin's cousins Gloria and Gene, and Barbara. Vin's parents were not there. Mildred managed to convince John to let her be present at St. Peter's Church in Belleville, but she was forbidden from attending the reception. A photograph taken inside the church shows Mildred there, beautifully attired in a v-neck dress, with a huge corsage and small pill-box hat. Her white-gloved hands are clasped together in front of her, holding a small purse that matches her dress. She is gazing over at my mother as if wishing she could only be a part of the happy bride's future life with her only son.

Despite the nearly empty pews inside the church and the pouring rain outside, the small dinner celebration was a joyous affair. Formal photographs were taken in front of the hearth in the front room of the Mayfair. The bride and groom sipped sparkling burgundy out of bowl-shaped glasses, and fed each other slices of the tiny but beautifully adorned white wedding cake. The loving gazes and broad smiles in their photographs carry no hint of what had happened just before the reception.

After the walk down the steps of St. Peter's in Belleville and getting into the black sedan driven by Vin's cousin Gene, Sandy announced that there was one stop she wanted to make before going to Mayfair Farms.

"Vin, we need to go see your father."

"Why, sweetheart? He's the one who refused to come to the wedding."

"I know. But he should still have the chance to see his only son on his wedding day."

"San, it's raining. Let's just go to the reception."

"No, Vin. This is the right thing to do. Gene, please take us to their house."

They pulled up to the small red brick house at 38 Mountainview Avenue in East Orange. The rain was dripping off the portico above the front door. Vin helped Sandy out of the car, with one hand on his umbrella and one hand guiding her safely onto the sidewalk. Choosing one of the twin sets of steps up to the door, Sandy held on to the wrought iron railing so as not to slip. Vin did his best to maneuver his umbrella to keep his bride dry. The couple found themselves standing together for the first time at John and Mildred's doorstep. They rang the doorbell.

Mildred had not yet had the chance to change out of the dress and hat she had worn to the church, and her surprise at seeing them at her doorstep was evident.

"Hi, Mom." Sounding less than convinced, Vin told her, "We've come to see Dad."

She was frozen in the doorway, conflicted between her own instincts and the reality of her husband's ways.

"Mom," Sandy had decided this was the only proper thing to call her mother-in-law, "this is our wedding day. We wanted to come see Dad before we leave on our honeymoon."

She looked at her son's new wife, marveling at her confidence and determination. Mildred nodded and went to get John.

Standing just inside the door, Sandy tried not to think about the only other time she had been at the house, alone, dressed in her favorite chiffon dress and wide-brimmed hat. She had been so anxious to win the hearts of Vin's parents that day. With Vin by her side this time, she was hopeful of a much better outcome.

Vin did not appreciate his status as visitor at a place where he and his wife should enter freely. This house, which his parents had moved into shortly after he met Sandy, was full of needless arguments in his mind, doused with drama and painful conflict. He had decided to put it behind him when he left for the last time. He greatly admired Sandy for her determination to mend things with his father, but wanted to get on with their life together.

Then they saw Mildred coming back to the door. She was alone.

Sandy modeling

Sandy with Bob Hope in Las Vegas, 1948

Sandy and Vin in Belmar on the Jersey Shore, 1954

Sandy and Vin with Barbara at Branchbrooke Park, 1955

At the church, from left: Mildred, Vin, Barbara, Sandy, Timmi Ritchie

Vin and Sandy, married!

Vin and Sandy on their honeymoon

At the Trevi Fountain, Rome, 1961

Burning the mortgage of the Cape house

Vin and Sandy in Hawaii

The five siblings singing to Sandy (or at least trying!) on her 75th birthday. From left: Don, Lynn, Kathy, Barbara, John, Vin at the piano, 2001

The entire family gathers for Vin and Sandy's 50th wedding anniversary, 2005

CHAPTER TWELVE

Family

I have a postcard written by my mother dated July 9, 1956, with a photograph of Rocky Mountain National Park, Colorado. It was posted from Cheyenne, Wyoming, and addressed to Mr. and Mrs. J. Apruzzese, 28 Mountainview Ave., East Orange, N.J.

> *Hi Mom and Dad,*
>
> *Spent week-end here with another couple. We all went horse-back riding, boating and ate all meals in open again. Even cooked chicken and corn. Went swimming and had a perfect time. Barbara really loved every second. Such beautiful scenery. Took films. Will write soon. Spent the 4th fishing. Busy, busy.*
>
> *Love,*
> *Sandy, Vin and Barby*

During their honeymoon in Bermuda, Vin had received his final orders to report to active duty in Cheyenne, Wyoming, effective January 1 of 1956. So just six months after their wedding, Sandy, Vin, and Barbara set out for cowboy country. I don't know exactly how many postcards and letters my mother wrote to John and Mildred while they were stationed out West, but she did her best to write to them every week despite her father-in-law's refusal to acknowledge her. Vin and his father had not spoken for over a year, and her letters and postcards were never answered. But Sandy would not be complicit in allowing the gulf in the relationship to expand, and hoped that keeping John and Mildred abreast of their lives would somehow keep them all connected. There was so much to tell them about the magical time they were experiencing at Warren Air Force Base.

Vin was working in the office of the judge advocate, which handled all criminal cases involving any of the twenty-one thousand military personnel on the base. All recommendations for action had to be made by the staff judge advocate and then signed off by the base commander. The appointed staff judge advocate at the time was a retired bombardier with impressive combat experience who happened to have a legal degree but absolutely no experience practicing law. He knew he needed help on the legal side of things, and quickly appointed Vin as his top assistant. In this role, Vin was the one to take all recommended legal activity to the base commander, putting him in an excellent position to be noticed by the senior officers on the base.

Sandy and Vin were making themselves known in many other ways as well, often due to Sandy's creative prowess. They entered several costume contests on base, as cannibals in one turn and scarecrows the next. The scarecrow costume was so realistic that another couple had to drive Vin and Sandy to the party with their broomstick arms sticking out the car windows on either side. They took home the best costume honors that night. Sandy also won the base sewing contest by fashioning a red wool shirt for Vin that he wore for years afterward. Sandy put her sewing expertise to more practical uses as well, continuing to sew all of her and Barbara's dresses and coats, making them two of the best-dressed yet least expensively attired girls on the base.

The Christmas house outdoor decorating contest was another big event on the base. Vin, Sandy, and Barbara's initial home was in a section called Wherry Housing. It was a one-story structure with a brick foundation and cement walls, essentially "a box with four rooms," my father tells me. For the contest, they flanked one of their windows with two evergreens adorned with large shiny snowflakes. The candles in the window flickered behind two life-size cardboard carolers that Sandy had made, holding their music and singing with their mouths in a cherubic '0' shape. Vin poured boiling water onto the front lawn the night before the contest to get the carolers properly staked into the frozen ground. He then rigged a stereo out the window to a speaker on the lawn that played beloved Christmas carols for the passersby. A portable TV was their first-place prize.

Sandy's greatest decorating feat came when she and one of the other wives took on the job of decorating the officers' club for a New Year's party in honor of the base commander. To create the feeling of a night club, they brought in huge urns and several fountains. But Sandy had a more extensive vision for the space, wanting to create the feel of a magical indoor forest. Because of Vin's relationship with the base commander, they arranged to have a truck full of branches gathered from around the base. These Sandy spraypainted a glittery white. Filling the room, the birch-like trees were covered with fresh grapes and white twinkling lights. No one had ever seen anything quite like it, and the base commander decided afterward that the young Apruzzese duo could do no wrong.

Vin marveled at his wife's talents, but was not surprised given the creative touch she had brought even to their first dinner party in East Orange. Shortly after moving into their Ampere Parkway apartment, Sandy had mentioned her idea of filling the false fireplace in their little apartment with lemon leaves, and how pretty it would look to place a single rosebud in a bud vase on the bureau in their bedroom. Rushing home from work on the day of the party, Vin bounded up the stairs with an armful of lemon leaves and a single rosebud, not understanding Marie Viscardi's chuckles as he rushed past her. He arrived home to find the fireplace already full, and the bud vase already displaying a rose. From then on, he left the details of entertaining in the hands of his capable wife.

Sandy must surely have written to John and Mildred about the cocker spaniel they had bought for Barbara, named Colonel. Colonel quickly made friends with a visiting toy beagle who would set up camp on their yard, sometimes for two weeks at a time, playing with Colonel (and likely eating the many treats that Barbara could not resist giving to him). He had no tag on his collar, so there was no owner to call and alert about the dog's whereabouts. After several of these extended visits, Vin had the idea of putting a tag on the dog with the name "Vin Apruzzese" and their home phone number. Sure enough, the next time the beagle wandered home, the owner immediately called, furious that anyone would have the gall to put their own name and number on his dog's collar. Vin quickly countered that if he cared about his dog, he should put on a tag of his own. The beagle didn't come back after that.

Sandy likely wrote about riding horses out onto the plains for Sunday morning pancake breakfasts and about "Frontier Days," when Barbara would delightedly dress up in full cowgirl regalia. She must have sent some of the many press clippings that mentioned Vin's appearance in "The Tender Trap" at Cheyenne's Little Theater. The comedy, put on by a combination of professional actors, members of the United Airlines Stewardess School, and officers from the Warren Air Force Base, was about the hilarity that ensues when a confirmed bachelor, played by Warren's Robert Borod, is visited by a married college friend. Perhaps she included the review written in the May 10, 1956, edition of the *Wyoming Eagle*, which stated:

> *The role of the visiting buddy was played by Vin Apruzzese, like his colleague of the evening, an officer at Warren and an equally welcomed addition to Little Theater. The role of both male leads was made to order for lively and unsubtle acting and both Borod and Apruzzese come to the head of the class of Cheyenne amateurs who believe properly dished-up ham is still the prize plate of any amateur production.*

I greatly doubt that she wrote to Vin's parents about the article that was written one year later about her as the "Warren-ality of the Month" in the *WoW (Warren Officer's Wives) Newsletter*. The author begins the article by acknowledging a certain amount of hubbub that preceded Sandy's arrival at the base fifteen months earlier because the wives had heard she was a model. They all found this "fascinating" and worried what to wear to meet her. The article went on to say:

> *Of course, all this will seem ridiculous to all who know her now. Of course she was perfectly but casually dressed and continued to put us at ease by her sincerity, joining in equally with our 'humdrum' conversation. Nothing was ever mentioned of her career...*

and you know, I think that was the last time I ever associated Sandy with anything more glamorous than her engaging personality and her ability to make you feel more important than she.

After a brief bio of Sandy's life and career, the article closes by saying that Sandy's modeling days are behind her, "and her only desired careers now are homemaking and babies. Good luck Sandy...thanks for showing us a glamorous model can also be a competent and versatile housewife and friend."

If she wrote in one of her letters about Barbara's holy communion, I wonder if she told Vin's parents that Barbara, looking proud and beautiful in her white communion dress after the service, ran through a plate glass door, severing the main artery in her arm. Despite the attempts of Sandy's mother, who was visiting for the occasion, to apply pressure to the wound and stem the bleeding, the doctors told Sandy that her instinct to ignore all stop signs and red lights on the way to the hospital probably saved her daughter's life. I'm sure she wouldn't have included the fact that Vin was at an important convention in New Jersey at the time.

I also wonder if any of her letters mentioned either of her two pregnancies or her two subsequent miscarriages. Sandy must have been so hopeful that a grandchild of his own might break John's cruel silence. The agony of irretrievable plans and dreams that come in the form of a lost child must have surely been painful enough without the disappointment of also losing the hope of potential reconciliation.

But she kept writing, surely penning many more postcards like the one from Rocky Mountain National Park, sharing exciting and mundane details from places like Yellowstone, Mount Rushmore, and the Badlands of South Dakota. Sandy wanted to be sure that Vin's parents were included in all the activities that were shaping their first years of married life. She had not given up hope that they would somehow come around and welcome them back into their life. She had thought it might take a child. She didn't know what else might as dramatically break the ruthless silence between father and son.

And then Vin received a call from one of his cousins. His mother had been diagnosed with breast cancer and was undergoing a mastectomy. Vin got on the first flight to Newark he could find. Walking down the corridor toward his mother's room, he was not at all sure what to expect. Hearing loss aside, his mother had always been a healthy and strong woman. It was his father he had always worried might suddenly collapse, not his vibrant mother.

Vin stood at the doorway of her room. She was asleep. She did not look as wan or feeble as Vin had been worried she might. Despite the wires and tubes all around her, she looked like someone who was finally drifting off after a restless night without sleep. John was sitting by her bedside. He looked older than Vin had remembered, less animated, with worry pulling on his shoulders and loosening his face.

"How is she?"

John looked up and then back at his wife.

"They say the operation went well, grazie a Dio."

Vin walked to the other side of the bed. He surveyed his mother's face, looking for reasons to feel optimistic. He bent down and kissed her forehead. When he sat down, he took her right hand in his.

"Hi, Mom. I'm here."

The two men sat watching Mildred sleep for several minutes. John finally broke the silence.

"Mio figlio, how about we go and get a bite to eat? You must be hungry after your long trip."

Vin looked up at his father. "Okay, Dad. That sounds great."

Walking out of the hospital room together, John put his hand on Vin's back. "I want to hear all about Wyoming."

They shared dinner together that night, talking about life in the service, business at the tavern, family news, and recovery plans for Vin's mother. It was as if nothing difficult had ever transpired between them.

Vin stayed in New Jersey until he was convinced that his mother was stable and moving in the right direction toward recovery. On his flight home, he smiled at the blessing of a family that was fully intact for the first time in years. His new family in Wyoming, anxiously awaiting his return, and his family in New Jersey were no longer at odds with each other, no longer tearing him in two. He was no longer behind his own goal line. He felt like a running back who had just broken the last tackle and was sprinting down the field.

CHAPTER THIRTEEN

Cape Cod

After that day in the hospital, not only did Vin's relationship with his father pick up right where it had left off, but John treated Sandy like the daughter-in-law he had always wanted. Whether it was the indisputable fact that the world had not crashed down on his son after marrying a divorced woman, that he saw something of himself in this independent and determined woman, or that John simply couldn't resist a woman whose love of family was stamped upon every letter she sent to them, he understood what a perfect wife she actually was for his only son. For the rest of his life, he "couldn't have loved Sandy more," says my father, and his generosity knew no bounds.

On Vin's next trip home from Wyoming to touch base with important contacts in New Jersey's legal scene, his mother was fully recovered and he stayed with his parents on Mountainview Avenue. When he arrived, John surprised him with an incredible gift. He told Vin to pick out a brand-new car.

"I figured you three could use a new car out there. You can drive it back and surprise Sandy!"

Vin had never had a new car before. He was dumbfounded. He chose a 1957 Dodge station wagon, and drove it back to Wyoming, surprising Sandy and Barbara equally when he arrived.

When Sandy and Vin moved back from Wyoming in the fall of 1957, they were invited to stay with John and Mildred while they looked for a new place to live. Sandy readily agreed. If the sudden switch from outcast to temporary resident in the Apruzzese home ever bothered her, she never let on. And if she worried that living there while pregnant might make the situation any less comfortable, she handled it with her usual grace. Rather than feel wary or skeptical about finally being welcomed across the threshold of the Apruzzese home, she simply embraced the invitation and approached it as a fresh start. Sandy and Vin stayed there through the birth of the baby. They named him John.

When Sandy and Vin finally did find the house they wanted to buy, on Lawn Ridge Road in South Orange, Vin only had two thousand dollars to put toward a deposit. His father didn't hesitate to loan him ten thousand dollars to put toward the house, interest-free. But the most important loan he ever made to his son was more than a decade later, for a summer house on Cape Cod.

Sandy knew she wanted to be in Chatham ever since their first visit to the Cape in 1961. They were invited by Bill Wachenfeld, a lawyer from Lum, Fairlie, with two other couples for Memorial Day weekend. That Saturday, they boated out of Ryder's Cove to North Beach, which my father described as "the most private and uncrowded beach we had ever seen." On the way back, they noticed the homes on the bluff to their left, never imagining that they would someday host a mortgage-burning party on one of those lawns.

Interestingly, Sandy's appendix burst that first weekend, requiring a ten-day hospital stay. This gave Vin plenty of time between hospital visits to tour the Cape and appreciate its differences from the familiar Jersey Shore. That visit cemented the idea of the Cape as the summer spot for them. On a recommendation from their friends the Bensons, they began to rent in Brewster Park, where the tide would go out a mile or more, offering endless hours of skim boarding and playing in the sand for my brothers. My mother could watch over them from the expansive deck and keep an eye on her napping toddler, my sister Lynn, at the same time.

While Vin was ready to buy in Brewster, Sandy still thought Chatham was the better location, and when a white colonial on Pleasant Bay came on the market in 1968, Sandy fell in love with it the minute she walked in. Their vision of a simple "sweep out" on the beach was quickly replaced by a grand old house from 1789 with original moldings and wide board floors. It stood on a fifty-foot bluff overlooking the bay, North Beach, and the ocean beyond. The negotiated price was higher than what they had paid for their primary residence in New Jersey, and Vin couldn't make the needed down deposit without help from his father. He never told his father the actual price of the house, fearing that that would kill the deal, but John happily leant the twenty thousand dollars his son needed to put together a forty-thousand-dollar deposit, agreeing to let Vin pay him interest this time. John was impressed by the type of people who had chosen Chatham as a summer location, including a Fortune 500 CEO with whom Vin had become friendly, and John was eager to help his son join that kind of crowd. Ironically, this same friend worried that Vin's eyes for real estate were bigger than his financial stomach and actually called him to advise him not to "go over the deep end."

But the now-parents of five somehow knew that it would be a place whose value would far outweigh any monetary calculation. It was the place all us kids couldn't wait to get to once school ended and the U-Haul was packed to the gills for the long trip north, wondering how many days it would take that year for our bare feet to toughen. It was a place whose doors were constantly open to visitors of all ages, local or distant, from my brother's best high school friend who would turn up for days at a time in between his tennis tournaments and my sister's college friends who called our house "Camp A" to my parents' friends who would regularly stop in for an impromptu hello. Our kitchen was a revolving door of enthusiastic visitors.

The Cape house was truly Sandy's domain from Memorial Day until Labor Day, and her crowning achievement as a home creator. She would spend hours weeding, planting, and nurturing every flower in a garden that was understated in its beauty because of the artistry of its caretaker, and appeared un-fussed over because of the diligence that went into its care. Similarly, every room of the house would have you notice the blues of the sky more than any wall color or window trim. And you couldn't help but feel the positive energy cultivated within the house as much as you would notice the stunning view beyond.

Somehow, Sandy managed to keep the refrigerator stocked with everything her growing children were determined to devour during three meals a day, plus enough gourmet ingredients at the ready for an impromptu dinner party or beach barbecue.

Vin commuted to the Cape on weekends. An example of his determination to utilize business to facilitate life, Vin eventually acquired a small twin-engine plane for the law firm, which not only ensured his timely response to geographically dispersed clients, for whom every hour of delay in tackling serious labor disputes could mean the loss of millions of dollars, but enabled him to get to the Cape on Fridays by dinner time and to stay until early Monday morning. Friday night dinners were a highlight of the week, more often than not a feast of fresh fish and steamed corn with all of us around our bright green dining room table. Sandy had the inspiration to resurrect their first dining room table from New Jersey by covering the unimpressive piece of furniture in a color one might associate with vintage Lily Pulitzer fabric. My brothers did the honors, and ensured the staying power of the green paint with at least nine coats of polyeurothane. A spectacular arrangement of hydrangeas would adorn the table, glass hurricanes sheltering candles on either side. We would usually linger at the table long after the food was gone, telling stories and filling the room with laughter. Tackling the pile of dishes in the kitchen was a group effort, synchronized to the latest album in favor. One of us would inevitably discover the charred loaf of bread in the oven, the only recurring flaw we could find in my mother's culinary prowess.

Cape Cod summer days usually started at the tennis court. We had just enough land across the road from our house for half of a tennis court. Our neighbors had enough room for the other half, so we jointly built a tennis court with the net at the property line. Kids and adults from both houses would wander over to the court as they woke up, cereal bowls or coffee cups in one hand, sneakers in the other. Doubles teams, of all ages, were formed and disbanded throughout the morning. Those not playing at any given time were unofficial line judges and scorekeepers or worked on a *New York Times* crossword puzzle in the shade. Sandy would keep everyone hydrated with an igloo full of iced tea and lemonade infused with fresh mint from the garden.

The court was transformed every Labor Day weekend into center court of the Cotchpinicut Tournament. Started as a simple round robin that involved several local couples in a fun day of competitive tennis, it culminated as a highly anticipated, multi-generational tournament that spread across three courts in town. Pairings were announced a day or two before the tournament, with all players eager to have their names engraved on the winning silver bowl that year and gain an invitation to the "Breakfast of Champions" the following morning. But everyone was really in it for the awards dinner. Alternating between our house and our neighbors' house, it was a night of fantastic food and outrageous awards. Sandy would cook for days to prepare for the event; fresh gazpatcho at lunch and sausage and pepper casserole at dinner were annual staples on the menu. No one coveted the Champion's Cup as much as they coveted a hilarious prize given for a questionable character trait or serious flaw in their tennis game. A ball and chain might go to the worst foot-fault offender one year and a newly engaged young player the next. Nothing went unnoticed by the comedic eyes of the tournament's "executive committee."

Before the sun reached its noon pinnacle most summer days, the group at the court would migrate toward North Beach. The boat would be loaded with towels, beach chairs, a little hibachi grill, and enough food and drink for a small mobile feast. We would take *Skookum* from our side of the bay across to North Beach and then trek across the three or four hundred yards to the ocean side for the afternoon, meeting up with several other families by simply spotting the collection of familiar boats that marked that day's chosen location. Sandy had always thought of everything needed, from sun tan lotion and boogie boards to potato salad and heated sauerkraut to go with the hamburgers and hotdogs. The set-up would have been impressive for any given day. What was impressive was that we made this trek almost every day.

After outdoor showers and pulling on wool sweaters to protect our crispy skin from the chill of dusk, the sun would turn the bay into a reflecting pool of orange and gold. Vin would inevitably put Frank Sinatra on the stereo and wrap his arm around his bride's waist behind the sink, or lead her by the hand over to a slightly larger patch of hard wood floor. And they would dance.

And they weren't the only ones to dance in that house. Frank Sinatra would often be followed by a more current beat, the rest of the family spinning around the floor of the "great room," Sandy always wanting to learn the latest moves. These impromptu dance parties were the prelude to several engagement parties, one complete with flying paper plates in place of the real plates typically broken for celebrations in the Greek tradition my brother John married into, and three picture-perfect weddings.

In the end, not only did the house on the Cape turn out to be the best financial decision Vin and Sandy ever made, it was their best life decision. My father describes Cape Cod as "the centerpiece of our lives, our family, and our children. It is more like home than any other place we have ever lived."

As he writes these last words, a shadow moves across the paper and pulls my father off the bluff in Cape Cod and back to Las Vegas.

"Sir," says the young waiter in blue shorts and pressed white shirt. "Our cocktail snack menu is now available from our pool bar. Can I get you anything?"

My father looks up and realizes that the sun has shifted its position from the right side of his umbrella all the way over to the left side as he has been writing, and it is threatening to peak below the canvas at any moment.

"Just a bit more water, please," he says, shaking out the hand that has been grasping his gold pen all day.

He senses that his legs are as stiff from sitting as his hand is from writing. He stands up to stretch his legs and takes his time getting to a fully straight stance. He looks around the pool area and doesn't recognize anyone from when he first arrived. The scene has shifted form young families cooling off in the heat of the day to couples gathering for cocktails and dips in the hot tub. He decides that he has written enough for today. What he needs is a good meal in a well air-conditioned restaurant and a solid night's sleep before catching his early morning flight home.

CHAPTER FOURTEEN

Heading Home

Four days after arriving in Las Vegas, my father waits to board the plane back to Florida. He is anxious to get back to Naples to see Sandy. He hasn't been apart from her for this long in months. He needs to see her to know that she is doing alright.

He hands his boarding pass to the woman standing by the podium. As she scans his ticket, he barely hears her say, "How are you today, sir?" He distractedly replies, "Oh, fine, thanks." Nothing like the time their flight home from Scotland was delayed and he entertained fellow passengers by showing off his newly purchased "Sherlock Holmes" hat and buying drinks for any takers with unspent Scottish coins. The appreciative crew asked if he and my mother "wouldn't mind moving up to first class" to help to alleviate an oversold situation in coach. They happily obliged.

Finding his aisle seat on this much more ordinary flight, he puts his newspaper on the seat next to him with his briefcase, more of a leather pouch than a hard case and nothing like the

117

huge accordion cases he used to lug around in the height of his career. But even in retirement, there is always something to review, finance reports for an upcoming hospital board meeting or a letter that needs a response. This time, he takes out the fifteen or so handwritten pages from the day before and begins to reread some of it:

As I tried to get my wife into the shower, she steadfastly resisted and said, "I want to go home." She repeated it several times, yet we were in our home. I was puzzled.

Such is the state of a dementia victim, I later came to learn from the Altzheimer's Support Network, where she is seeking, searching, yearning for that place of comfort, security and warmth, perhaps peace of mind, that is eluding her/them. It is not really a physical place but they call it home.

It is inexplicable how devastating a blow those words are, coming from your loved one, when you understand what they mean. The depth of despair is recognized and the futility of changing it sets in as the disease moves slowly but inexorably onward as the journey continues.

What will our future life be like? When did it begin and how will it end? Why did it happen to her, to us? What must be done to deal with it? These thoughts and more roll through your mind while you try to adjust to meet the needs of your life partner.

For us, from the moment of our miraculous meeting, our stormy but love-filled courtship, a glorious fifty-two-year marriage, five children, the experience of traveling the world, frequently with our children, the deep intensity of our love and fulsome happiness, all of these must be understood to appreciate the enormity of loss felt by the caring partner, and as time progresses, the unknowing victim.

"Please buckle your seatbelt, sir," says the flight attendant as he walks by for final checks. Vin puts his papers down next to him, reaches into his front pocket for his phone, turns it off, and places in on top of his papers. He buckles his seatbelt and notices the other passengers for the first time. A young couple is sitting across the aisle from him, the man in the window seat, the woman barely occupying her middle seat as she leans into him, hands clasped together on his lap. My father thinks of all the incredible trips he and his bride had taken over the years. He hadn't had the time to write about any of it yet. So many wonderful places, so much great food, great wine, fun friends, unforgettable memories. He begins to replay their first trip to Europe in his mind.

True to his word to use work as a means to enjoy life, this trip was en route to the 1961 International Labor Law Society conference in Lyon, France. While many colleagues arrived one day before the four-day meeting and scurried back directly afterward, Vin and Sandy decided to make a full adventure out of it. Their first destination was Positano, Italy, where they stayed for four days at the Buca di Bacco on the beach. Ah, Positano, a place they would return to many times, sometimes just the two of them, sometimes with friends, all subsequent visits staying at the famed San Pietro Hotel. They loved to tell people about their favorite small bistro perched on the edge of the beach and the night they asked their waiter, "Mario, dove la luna? (Where is the moon?)" He smiled at his loyal guests, "E venuta, e venuta" (It's coming, it's coming), as if he was in possession of the key to a vault and was holding it back.

After leaving Positano for the first time, the pair spent a few days in Capri then traveled by way of Naples to Rome. Vin Buinno from Lum, Fairlie & Foster had told his friend that they must go to Pisettos on Piazza Navona to taste their cannelloni. Upon leaving the restaurant at about 10:30 p.m., they spontaneously jumped into a horse-drawn carriage for a ride. Sensing the couple's exuberance, the driver took them on a complete tour of the city, past such unforgettable landmarks as the Coliseum, the Forum, and to the famed Trevi Fountain. He snapped a photo of the couple in front of the Trevi Fountain, she smiling brightly in a spectacular green rain cape, he throwing a coin behind them for good luck. You would never guess by their animated stances that the photo was taken past midnight.

Venice was next. After a layover in Milan during which they wound up on separate platforms and almost missed their train, their entrance into the city of water was spectacular. They left the train station by gondola, the sun setting over the canals. The tenor on a neighboring boat made their romantic ride the perfect entrance into the city. One night after dinner, they walked the three blocks from their hotel to St. Mark's Square, a large piazza bordered by the Church of St. Mark and long rows of elegant buildings all sharing three stories of endless arches. Allegedly dubbed the "drawing room of Europe" by Napoleon, the square is an impressive sight by daylight. But on that night they chanced upon an eighty-piece orchestra playing beneath the yellow and orange glow of thousands of candles flickering off the walls of the square.

After a visit to Geneva via Zurich and a breathtaking drive through the Alps, Vin and Sandy finally arrived in Lyon for the start of the conference. DeGaule was in power at the time, and the couple was sorely disappointed to see that the antipathy between the French and Americans ensured that the Americans on the trip got all the worst rooms in the hotel. After such a glorious tour about Europe, more than a couple of days in the uninspiring city of Lyon seemed like a waste, and so Vin and Sandy left the conference early and headed for Paris. Sandy's favorite uncle, George Jordan, and his wife, Aunt Helen, were there at the time, and they took in the sights and sounds of Paris together, happily capping off their trip in the city of love.

My father shifts in his seat and smiles at the memory. Whenever it was pointed out to him that this kind of four- or five-day "business trip" must have taken them at least three weeks, he was always quick to respond, "Oh, at least. It was fabulous!" They did this every year for thirty five years, often joined by other conference-attending couples, many of whom became lifelong friends. There were too many trips to Europe to count, and travels as far as Hungary, Russia, Japan, and Hong Kong. Not to mention countless vacations with the family, skiing in the Rockies and the Alps, sailing in the Caribbean, a trip on the QE2. So many memories.

My father doesn't realize he has fallen asleep until the wheels of the plane suddenly screech onto the landing strip and jolt him awake. He blinks in the bright yellow glare pressing up against the plane's oval windows. The heat visibly rising up off the tarmac tells him he is back in Florida. He checks his watch and notes that the plane is on time. He figures he could be through the airport and to his car in about twenty minutes, which, depending on traffic between Fort Meyers and Naples, would probably get him to Sandy in just over an hour.

As he pulls onto the highway to head back toward Naples, he wonders what her reaction will be when she sees him. Will she be angry with him for going away? Will she have a sense of how long he has been gone? He hopes she hasn't been anxious because he has been away, although the possibility that she hasn't even noticed his absence is equally wrenching.

In the span of a lifetime, things had deteriorated so quickly. But in other ways, watching his bride sink into dementia had been like watching an oncoming collision in slow motion, and being powerless to deflect the impact or decrease its force. He had always been the one to respond in a crisis, to spring into action and get things set right. There was a resourceful solution to everything. Or at least there always had been.

He would never forget the first time she got lost. She had gone to her regular hair appointment and come back in tears. She hadn't been able to find the salon. And then she had gotten so turned around, she almost couldn't find her way home. It was hard to sort through what had been worse: the reality that this highly independent woman had gotten lost less than five miles from home, the fear that must have risen up in her esophagus like bile from knowing that something was wrong, or the glare of anger in her eyes when he took her keys a few days later and told her that he couldn't let her drive alone anymore.

"Do something, Vin," she implored. "Why don't you do something to fix this?"

He called every doctor he knew and asked for advice and references. They saw every specialist that could possibly have answers. There would be no easy diagnosis, no obvious pharmaceutical regime to offer a cure.

"Promise me you won't tell anyone," she would say to him. "Especially the children."

But as time went on, the telltale signs increased and were impossible to ignore. Her extreme agitation if he left the house for any length of time, the note in the kitchen reminding her where he had gone, forgotten as soon as he walked out the door. His taking her with him to watch his weekly tennis match, but being unable to keep her from wandering onto the court as if she were simply crossing a room to be closer to him. Her taking her panties out of the washing machine and putting them in the microwave. Turning the light on every twenty minutes or so between 1:00 a.m. and 4:00 a.m., insistent it was time to get up. His search around the house for the TV remote, only to find it in the car door. Ten minutes after returning home from a drive, hearing her agitation kick in again. "Let's go. Where should we go?"

Then there were the phone conversations with their children on the phone, like the one regarding plans for Thanksgiving in Naples.

"Will you be driving here for Thanksgiving?"

"No, Mom. We'll be coming by plane."

"Oh? Where are you right now?"

"We're in Boston, Mom, so we'll be flying to Florida."

"Oh, I just thought...since it's such a quick drive to the Cape."

Everyone told him that he shouldn't try to care for her all on his own, that his bleeding ulcers were a bad sign. A woman at the Alzheimer's Network, named Marianne, helped him navigate his early days of confusion and despair, and even helped him find someone to come to the house to help. She introduced him to Mary, a lovely woman who had lived through her own husband's dementia-driven decline and wanted nothing more than to ease the pain of other families experiencing the same agony. But whenever Mary was in the house, Sandy's paranoia kicked into full gear.

"I hear you talking in low voices to that woman when I'm not in the room. Why is she in my house? What's going on, Vin?"

And then the cruel loss of continence, stripping away the last layer of normalcy as painfully as ripping duct tape off a wound. Once the understanding of what was happening to her was gone, any attempt to help prevent or clean up after accidents became a daily struggle of personal privacy, an attempted loving act met with protest and shame-shielding anger.

Barbara moved into the house in Naples like an angel sent to hold up the walls of the house to keep them from caving in on his head. Her presence meant stealing an occasional nap, eating home-cooked meals instead of repeated take-out, handing off daily sheet and clothing sanitation to someone else's loving hands, and even getting out of the house for a walk. Most importantly, it meant staving off for a few precious months the unthinkable, moving Sandy into a full-time care facility. It was a decision that everyone else seemed to think inevitable, and that no one dreaded more than him.

He and Barbara took such pains to make her room at Terracina look like home. They had everything painted in blue hues and dimmers put on all the lights. The white wooden bed with lovely linens looked almost like her own. They made sure to put her lipsticks in her top bathroom drawer and the tiny wedding photo on her nightstand. They placed a silver-framed shot of the whole family together on a bookshelf, and tacked up a calendar full of grandkids.

But nothing could prepare him for the day it was time to move her there. Dr. Beckwith, an expert in these things, suggested that the best way to effect the transition from home into the facility would be to leave the house as if going on any normal outing, arrive at the facility as if it has always been home, introduce Sandy to a friendly staff member, and quietly step away, like a parent slipping out of the house while the baby is distracted by the sitter. The doctor explained that this kind of transition essentially bewilders the patient into tacit acceptance, avoiding the confusion and anxiety that can be caused by an emotionally charged event. The transition is further cemented, he counseled, by refraining from visiting for the first four or five days. What the doctor could not explain was how to stop everyone else's heart from shattering into pieces.

John came down to Naples to help with the move. Sandy would easily go anywhere with him with a smile and no questions, and as the oldest son, it was somehow decided that he could handle this role without falling apart. That morning he suggested they should go for a drive, and she happily complied, not in the slightest bit aware that she would be walking out of her own home forever.

Barbara snuck out of the house and headed to Terracina ahead of them to bring her robe and a few last-minute essentials to the room and to review the timing of the plan with Sarah and Millie, two key staff members who had taken a genuine interest in our family. Barbara double-checked that the door to the dementia wing would be unlocked and open so as to look like any other door. Everything took longer than anticipated, and before Barbara could exit the building, Sarah called her into the kitchen area to avoid being seen. Looking through a window out into the hall, she could see John coming, Sandy's arm holding his as they walked through the door of the dementia wing. She wanted so badly to hug her mother and "explain" what was happening. John was surely feeling much less steady on his feet than he looked. Thankfully, Millie was waiting for them.

"Mom, this is Millie."

"Hi Sandy. It's so nice to meet you. I've heard so much about you."

Sandy's reflex of returning a smile was still in evidence, but it had become less enthusiastic the less she could understand the context behind the friendly expression.

Taking Sandy's arm from John, Millie turned Sandy and began to guide her down the hall.

"We just need to take your blood pressure. Come right over here with me."

"Oh," Sandy said, and calmly allowed herself to be led down the hall toward the nurses' station, away from her son.

My father wasn't supposed to be there. He had agreed with Barbara and John that he would leave the house before any of them. They had hoped he would go to talk with Dr. Beckwith while the move was happening so as not to be alone. But how could he be so far away? He knew his emotions wouldn't make a smooth transition possible for Sandy, but he had to be near. So he drove to Terracina and parked within eyesight of the front door. He sat alone in his car as he watched John walk up the sidewalk with Sandy's arm in his. Sandy stopped for a while to admire the fountain in front of the building. Tears flowed over his smile— he had known she would think it was pretty. He saw John open the door for his mother and guide her inside. He watched the door close behind them. And with that, she was gone.

It took every bit of his strength not to rush out of the car, tell everyone he had make a mistake, and take her back home with him. I don't know how long he sat there before he could see the road well enough to drive away.

As my father pulls into that same parking lot after his flight from Las Vegas, he is shaking back that memory. He is excited to see my mother after four long days and doesn't want sadness to creep into their visit.

Her room is empty when he gets there, so he wanders the halls for a few minutes to find her, swerving to the right side of the hall to touch the edge of a table holding activity schedules and support group brochures, then cutting back across the hall to turn left down another corridor. He finds her sitting in a courtyard on a white bench. She is wearing one of the pink warm-up suits he had picked out for her, a sacrifice of fashion for comfort and warmth. Her silvery hair looks wispy in the light breeze. She is holding a Raggedy Ann doll one of the aides had given her, distractedly playing with the red braids.

"Hi, San." He bends down and kisses her forehead.

She looks up and smiles.

"Oh, there you are!" she says.

He sits down beside her and takes her hand in his. "How've you been, sweetheart?"

She looks at his face, as if searching for a clue to something she has forgotten.   "Oh, fine, fine."

"You look great, San," he says, and brings her hand to his lips for a kiss.

She furrows her brow as if she has just found the clue she had been searching for.

"Where have you been?"

"Remember?" he says. "I told you I had to go get some tests to make sure everything is still okay after my kidney operation."

"Oh," she says, stroking a braid.

He squeezes her hand and pats it. She looks at his hands and then up into his eyes with some surprise.

"Where have *you* been?" she asks.

"I had to go away for a few days, San. But here I am. It's good to see you."

He smiles at her, and she opens her eyes a bit wider, raises her eyebrows, and laughs a little.

"Oh, you," she says, waving her hand at him as if she has come late to the punch line of a joke.

She untangles her other hand from his and goes back to fumbling with the doll. Her movements seem frustrated, as if she wants to change something about the Raggedy Ann but isn't sure what.

He puts his hand on the back of her head, stroking her silky hair the way one might comfort a child. They sit on the bench together for some time, looking at the confines of the courtyard. There are three crisscrossing walkways with a small palm tree in the middle. They watch one patient push through on his walker and another shuffle along beside a visitor.

Just then her brow knits into the look of someone wrestling with a very complex problem. She looks up at her husband with questioning eyes.

"I want to go home," she says.

He takes her hand in his again and wills the water to stay behind his eyes.

"So do I, sweetheart," he says, looking back into her searching eyes. "So do I."

* * *

Acknowledgments

It turns out that writing a book, even one of few pages, is not as solitary a venture as I had imagined. There are so many people to whom I am grateful for their love, support, and input throughout the process.

First, a debt of gratitude to Dan for reigniting my long-held desire to write this story by opening my eyes to the new world of publishing. I might never have started without that inspiration.

To Debra and Ilona for reading my earliest chapters. Your encouraging words meant a lot to me.

To Nancy for lending your astute professional eye, which led me to reconsider some critical structural decisions.

To Molly, the unsuspecting and brave reviewer of the first complete draft. As such an avid reader, the specificity of what you liked was very validating.

To my friend Nora for your thorough and heartfelt reading. Every comment struck a chord in me, and your ideas helped me improve the book in really important ways.

To my husband. Thank you for your reading as an "insider" and giving me your gentle yet pivotal input. Mostly, I thank you for your unwavering support of this project from the outset. You are my biggest cheerleader in everything I do.

To Henry and George for your enthusiasm about "Mommy's book" and for putting up with me when my computer was too often on my lap.

To you, Dad, there is so much to thank you for. It is nearly impossible to pull stories out of the fog of time, dust them off, and bring color back to a tavern in Newark or the flush of a young woman's cheeks without the love and strength of someone who cherishes every moment of that life, the hard moments as well as the joyous ones, and understands that they are all important components of a rich and meaningful life. Thank you for reaching back into the corners of your life in such loving detail and always with great purpose. Thank you for your tireless reading and rereading of every page to make sure it all rang true. Most importantly, thank you for trusting me with the most important story of your life.

Lastly, my heart overflows with gratitude to you, Mom, for which words are woefully insufficient. You created home in my heart, architected out of love, reinforced with encouragement, windows thrown open to possibility. I miss you desperately, but know you are always with me in the birds and the chimes.

Made in United States
North Haven, CT
05 October 2021

10154253R00079